EXPLORER'S GUIDES

DALLAS & FORT WORTH WITHDRAWN

A Great Destination

1ST EDITION

DALLAS & FORT WORTH

A Great Destination

Laura Heymann and
Monica Prochnow

The Countryman Press
Woodstock, Vermont

LEFT: *The view of downtown Dallas from the Belmont Hotel.* MK Semos

Explorer's Guide Dallas & Fort Worth: A Great Destination
ISBN 978-1-58157-126-4

Interior photographs by the author unless otherwise specified
Maps by Erin Greb Cartogaphy, © The Countryman Press
Book design by Bodenweber Design
Composition by PerfecType, Nashville, TN

Published by The Countryman Press, P.O. Box 748, Woodstock, VT 05091

Distributed by W. W. Norton & Company, Inc., 500 Fifth Avenue, New York, NY 10110

Printed in the United States of America

10 9 8 7 6 5 4 3 2 1

We would like to thank
our families, friends, and colleagues
who gave their time, ideas, and support
to us during this project.

Dallas–Fort Worth Metroplex

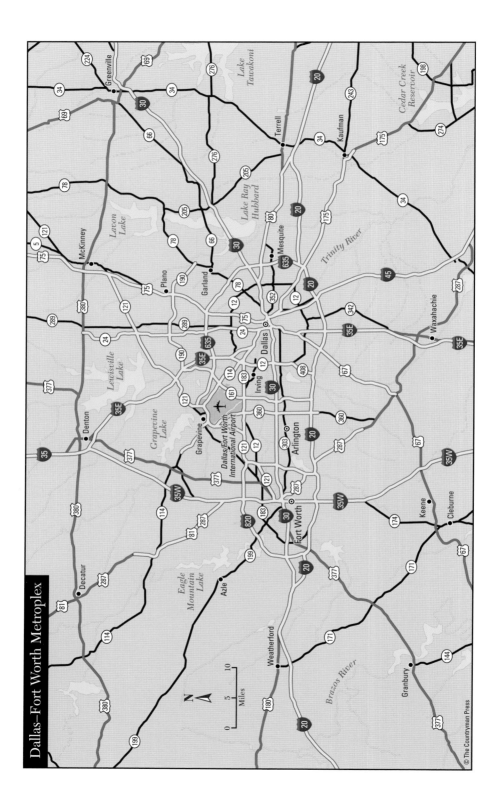

© The Countryman Press

Contents

Acknowledgments

We both know and love Dallas–Fort Worth, but the Metroplex is so large and complex that we would not have been able to research and visit the area or write this book without the help and support of many people. First, our gratitude goes to every person and organization that endured our interviews, entertained our requests, and graciously offered photos and information so that our efforts would be made that much easier.

A special thank-you goes to Kim Grant, our editor at The Countryman Press, whose patience with us, even during our suggested "check-in" dates, was undeservedly unwavering. Our gratitude to Kermit Hummel at Countryman, as well, who never doubted our abilities. Thanks to both of you, we were able to transform our far-fetched wish of writing a book into a reality. It is our hope that this book will make you proud.
—LH & MP

Thank you to my husband, Mike—you are my *favorite*, and I truly appreciate all you do for our family—you are a wonderful husband and father. To my kiddos, Victoria and Elias, I love you both bunches and thank you for always keeping me on my toes. I am so proud that of all the kids in the world, I have you. To my parents, David and Toni, thank you for always being supportive of my hair-brained projects, whether it's moving to Las Vegas, adopting a child, starting a business, or writing a book—y'all are awesome. To my friends, thank you for providing comic relief, always checking in with me, and offering fun suggestions for "book breaks." Monica, thank you for the invitation and the opportunity to work on this with you! And thank you for your hospitality in providing the perfect quiet place to write, since my house is a tornado of activity. Greg, you rock! Big shout-outs to the iPhone and Facebook—without them, I would have never gotten finished.

But in all seriousness, having grown up in DFW, I had been to many of the places mentioned in this book, but not in the last 20 years or so. In revisiting them with my family for the purposes of writing this book, I got to really see DFW again, through their eyes. And it was beautiful. I hope everyone who reads this book has a wonderful time here in my hometown—see you around!

xo, Laura

My gratitude extends to so many people who helped me with this book, directly and indirectly. Thank you to my colleagues and students (past and present) at Carter-Riverside High School who generously gave their recommendations and gave this book a jump start. Particular thanks goes to my adopted family in the English department, as well as Kristy, Raul, and Maria, and others too numerous to mention, who constantly checked on my sanity and reminded me to occasionally resurface for a gulp of fresh air. To my baby sister Taylor, who can accomplish anything, and to my dad, who always had faith in me. My gratitude goes to Bonnie and Crystal for their unrelenting friendship and for planting the idea of this book into my head. Thanks to Al, Irene, Susan, and Randy for their love. A nod also goes to my friends and professors at UTA who also offered suggestions and support. Of course, I would be remiss to not thank my dear friend and coauthor Laura and her hubby Mike, whose generosity and hospitality enabled me and my husband to come to Texas in the first place. And of course, my gratitude goes to the keeper of my heart and soul, Greg. You took on the world month after month and never complained, even when you should have, so I could be unencumbered when writing this book. I adore you for all that you are, and I couldn't possibly express how grateful I am for your unwavering love and support of me and this project. I hope I get to return the favor someday. I love you, Greg.

—MP

INTRODUCTION

I'm what you would call an accidental Texan. It was never my aspiration to move here, but I fell into it by life's circumstances. Oh, sure, I'd visited a couple of times and enjoyed myself, but to live in Texas? I would have never guessed it.

I had been laid off (again) as an editor/writer, this time from a job I actually liked. (Sigh . . .) My husband and I had been trying to leave Las Vegas, our hometown, for years, and I was convinced now more than ever that someone was trying to tell me something with all of the personal and professional roadblocks I had been encountering. I needed to make a life change, but I didn't know how or to what end.

My friend and former coworker Laura, who had moved back to her home state of Texas, told me how wonderful it was to be home and that I should consider moving there, too. I sent out a couple of résumés, some to places in Texas and others elsewhere, and the next day I received a call from some folks in Texas. I was on a plane and flying to an interview within a few days.

My husband, Greg, and I moved to Texas shortly thereafter, and it was the best thing for us. I have been at the same job for nearly five years—a surprise to anyone who had ever known me in my Las Vegas days. I bought a house, something I could have never done back home. I have friends, adopted "family," and even adopted children. I started a doctorate program at UTA, and my husband also went back to school to finish his degree. Texas has been good to us.

Texas represents a fresh start along a once-staid path. Who would have thought that moving three states eastward meant moving three steps forward? I love my new home, and I'm glad I'm here. I'm proud to be a Texan, and I feel fortunate.
—MP

I grew up in the suburbs of DFW—actually, I lived in the same house from the time I was brought home from the hospital until I left for college at 17 (I know, what a freak, right?). Off to a big-shot school to be a big-shot journalism major, I swore I would move to New York City or Chicago upon graduation and scoffed at the idea of ever gracing DFW with my presence again—I never wanted to be married, have kids, or be rooted anywhere (my extended family still likes to harass me about my longtime aversion to white picket fences).

After college, moving to Las Vegas wasn't exactly part of my master plan (single, age 22, and without knowing anyone in Nevada) but you see, in a post-9/11 NYC, every publication and ad agency I contacted was on a hiring freeze. My then-boss had an "in" for me in Las Vegas. . . . I took it, sight unseen. A couple years later, after working as a wedding planner at Caesars Palace and a graphic designer at a magazine (where I met Monica), I married my husband, who had a daughter back in Texas, so we decided we would build our life back here.

Build, have we ever! We got married, moved halfway across the country, got a puppy, bought a house, started new jobs and my husband's then-10-year-old daughter moved in with us, all within three months. I guess we figured, "Why stop there?" because we now have the same house, but different jobs, a 15-year-old daughter, a 12-year-old son, three dogs, and I've only just turned 30. I never would have guessed I'd have all this, and in DFW, to boot! Hey, everything's bigger in Texas, right?
—LH

How to Use This Book

This is the place in most guidebooks where the authors will give you rating systems or pricing guides, but we feel that modern technology has enabled travelers to be a bit savvier these days. Menus, hotel rates, and ticket prices are almost always online and vary greatly from one day to the next, but what the Internet does not give you, particularly in an area as large as the Dallas–Fort Worth Metroplex that has so much to offer, is a sense of direction and thoroughness.

The Metroplex is comprised of 110 separate communities spread throughout 12 counties and is home to over 6.5 million people. To limit this book to just the city of Dallas or just the city of Fort Worth is silly, especially when some of the major attractions, restaurants, sports stadiums, and even the primary airport are in neither Dallas nor Fort Worth. In fact, a person can drive a straight path on the same road for 15 minutes and unknowingly pass through eight cities.

As such, we have divided the Metroplex into five distinct regions: the Arlington area, the Dallas area, the Denton area, the Fort Worth area, and the Plano area. This, we believe, will help you determine where and how you spend your time and will help you navigate to areas beyond.

The Arlington area includes the southern and eastern portions of Tarrant County, as well as Johnson County.

Dallas includes Dallas County, Rockwall County, and Kaufman County.

Denton includes Denton County and Wise County.

Fort Worth includes Parker County and the bulk of Tarrant County.

Plano includes Collin County and Hunt County.

Organization

The nine chapters of this book are straightforward, but like the people who wrote it, it has moments when it is teeming with quirks and personality. Chapter 1 is a history of the Metroplex. The first segment covers the indigenous peoples that once populated the North Texas area, and the two remaining sections divide the region in half and cover the separate histories of Dallas and Fort Worth. As much as we wanted to, we decided it was physically impossible to provide a comprehensive history of the Metroplex and the smaller 110 communities within it.

Chapter 2 focuses on getting to DFW and maneuvering through the area. Chapter 3 features lodging options in the Metroplex. There are many hotel and motel chain rooms available, but we have focused on interesting boutique hotels, bed-and-breakfast inns, and grand luxury estates.

The fourth and fifth chapters offer vital information on the culture and dining in the area—the hallmarks for which a region is often judged. We are happy to say that the chapters on culture and restaurants, which also includes a section on food purveyors and listings for late-night hot spots, are two of the largest chapters in the book. That's great news, because we love our culture and we are unabashedly vocal about our love of good food, especially barbeque and Tex-Mex.

Chapter 6 covers sports, which rule in DFW. Sports in Texas are akin to Mom, apple pie, and, well, baseball in the rest of the country. We have it all—major-league football, basketball, baseball, hockey, soccer, golf, and a full roster of minor-league teams, college teams, and even some extremely impressive high school teams. Yes, we're serious about sports, even about our high school sports. *Friday Night Lights*, anyone?

The seventh and eighth chapters are devoted to recreation and shopping, which for some folks are the same thing. The recreation chapter focuses on family-friendly activities that include tours, areas for walking around, fun attractions and things for people to do and see, day trips to outlying areas, local and state parks, and area lakes. Shopping includes high-end locales and hidden gems.

Chapter 9 includes information on emergency services, child care, weather preparedness, and special needs services, and even contains a few words about the alcohol and tobacco laws.

Welcome to Dallas–Fort Worth!

HISTORY

Cities in Opposition

Tejas, a name from one of the local indigenous peoples, is translated as "friendly." Texans are proud of their reputation as being a friendly and hospitable people, and the denizens of the Dallas–Fort Worth area, in particular, are no different. But the history of both Dallas and Fort Worth do not always reveal a legacy of friendliness; in fact, the histories of these colorful cities often reveal a dark side, full of greed, murder, and other sinister dealings. Even in times when the people of either of these cities were not friendly to one another, they always embraced opportunity. The people of both Dallas and Fort Worth lived their lives as they chose but always with a gleaming eye gazing toward the future. The similarities between these two cities, however, end there.

Dallas and Fort Worth are only 35 miles apart from one another and are part of the same metropolitan area, yet they are miles apart in attitude and lifestyle. Dallas, or "Big D," is all about the image, the chic, and the fast pace. Fort Worth, or "Cowtown," is laid back, connects to its cowboy heritage, and is a bit slower. Dallas was built as an extension of an expanding East, and corporations and railroads came here to further build their existing mercantile and transportation empires; it has always looked eastward for inspiration. Fort Worth was intended, even before the first log was hewn, to be the demarcation line between the West and the end of "civilization." It truly was meant to be where the West began, and it has never lost that spirit, even as frontier moved past it. Ask residents of both cities if Texas is a western state or a southern state, and you might just get two different answers.

The Native Peoples

The earliest Texans are believed to be descendants of the various Asian groups that migrated across the Bering Strait and traveled south, venturing through Texas and onward into South America.

PLEISTOCENE AGE, 13,500 B.C.

About 12,000 years ago, the indigenous peoples were known to be large-game hunters. Their culture, one of nomadic hunters and gatherers, used spears to hunt the meat of woolly mammoths, mastodons, and giant buffalo and supplemented their diets with local

LEFT: *Esplanade at the Centennial* From the collections of the Texas/Dallas History and Archives Division, Dallas Public Library

roots, seeds, and berries. They continued living this way until the large animals suddenly died out when the climate changed around 7,000 years ago. Nonetheless, the humans survived and even thrived in their warmer, drier environs.

ARCHAIC PERIOD, 6000 b.c.

Smaller animals—buffalo, antelope, and deer—became the new prey. The indigenous peoples used spears with greater results, and they also began to harvest fruits and nuts, as well as eat mussels and other aquatic life from the Texas rivers.

LATE PREHISTORIC PERIOD, a.d. 700–1500

Around A.D. 700 people began to settle into communities and grow crops and local plants, which provided most of their diet. They began to use bows and arrows, enabling them to hunt both large and small game. Pottery was, for the first time, utilized for carrying water and cooking. These people were part of the pre-Caddoan tribes.

Making themselves at home

THE CADDOES

The Caddoes were the largest group to settle in the area, and they were a sophisticated society, complete with well-defined social strata and strong agricultural practices; they even participated in trade. The Alabama and Coushatta, both subgroups of the Caddoes, traveled from Alabama and settled along the Trinity River, which runs through the Metroplex, in the 1700s.

OTHER NATIVE GROUPS MOVE IN

The Apaches, known for their ferocity, moved in around the 1600s, and the Comanches, an equally fierce group, migrated during the 1700s into the area. The Comanches befriended the Kiowas, who moved to Texas in the late 1700s. The Wichitas also migrated to areas near present-day Dallas and were known for their handicrafts and produce farms.

EUROPEAN EXPLORATIONS AND CLAIMS

Territories within Texas were claimed and colonized by different groups—Spain in 1541 and France in 1685, both of which raced to claim Texas lands. France sold its landholdings to the United States in 1803, and the ill-defined boundary was not strongly upheld. To complicate matters, Cherokees settled on lands between the Trinity River and the Sabine River in East Texas, moving the Caddoes off their original lands. The Cherokees were among the "Five Civilized Tribes" to adopt agriculture and peacefully settle into the area. The Shawnee, Delaware, and Kickapoo Indians soon joined the Alabama-Coushatta peoples. Mexico entered a war for independence against Spain (1810–1821), and Mexico emerged as its own nation with many Texas territories still in its holdings. Land was cheap, and whites flocked to the area, outnumbering Hispanics four to one. Tensions grew between the two groups.

The battle of the Alamo in San Antonio occurred between Mexican and Texan soldiers in 1836, and Texas was granted, by written decree, freedom to make itself an independent nation. The Republic of Texas was born. The Texas Land and Emigration Company was hired to encourage settlement in the area and ran advertisements to lure people with the promise of good soil. Headed by W. S. Peters, the company was granted over 10 million acres of land. The Republic, at the time, had about 41 million acres, a sparse population, and no money—the Peters Colony was established.

WHERE THE EAST ENDS: DALLAS SETTLEMENT

The Peters Colony extended north to the Red River. Each eligible head of household (veterans of war) could claim first-class land grants, giving them 640 acres. Second-class land grants were given to single men or women who immigrated to the area after the Texas Declaration of Independence but before Oct. 1, 1837, and could claim 320 acres. Third- and fourth-class land grants were given to immigrants between Oct. 1, 1837 and Jan. 1, 1842. Widely advertised throughout the United States and Europe, Texas lands saw nearly 3,000 settlers move in.

JOHN NEELY BRYAN TAKES A LOOK, 1839

John Neely Bryan visited North Texas from Arkansas to survey the area. He examined the three forks of the Trinity as a possible location for a future trading post to serve both the native peoples and settlers; there he found an intersection where the native tribes traveled. This site was the easiest place to cross the river.

Bryan went home to finalize his affairs but returned to find the native peoples relocated from the area, as well as half the settlers. Instead, he changed his trading post plans and targeted an existing community about 22 miles northwest, Bird's Fort, for his future customer base.

Bryan worked for the Holland Coffee trading post on the Red River, where he bought and traded building parcels of land. Bryan listened to the rumors of vacant land in an area called Three Forks of the Trinity and saw opportunity.

STICKS AND STONES MAKE IT A TOWN, 1841

John Neely Bryan settled on the East Bank of the Trinity River, claiming the area with a stick and a few stones. Peter's Colony, on authority by the Republic of Texas seeking to expand settlement in Texas lands, lauded the successful creation of the new town, even though Bryan was essentially a squatter on colony land. Bryan appealed to the Bird's Fort residents to help him settle a separate town.

LEAVING THE BIRD'S NEST AND JOINING RANKS, 1842

The Beesman and the Gilbert families, who had problems with the indigenous people, left Bird's Fort and joined Bryan, and others followed. Bryan's largest challenge, however, was encouraging people to take a lot in his new town and not the free acreage from Peter's Colony land grants.

Settlement was not easy. While the townspeople were building homes and clearing the land for crops and animal pens, the transport of supplies and people posed a clear problem for Bryan. The two existing roads, the Preston Trail and the Central National Road, which led from Dallas to the Red River in the north, were primitive, at best.

FROM REPUBLIC TO UNION

In 1845, 29 out of 32 voters approved Texas's annexation to the United States. They believed it was time for Texas to sacrifice independence for the advantages that would come with joining its powerful neighbor, the United States.

There are a couple of tales of how Dallas was named. First is the story of Charity Gilbert, a member of the founding families: Gilbert reportedly won a city-naming contest, suggesting the name of "Dallas," in honor of Commodore Alexander Dallas, a naval hero believed to have fired the first shot in the War of 1812. Another story is that the town was named after George Mifflin Dallas, James K. Polk's vice president, who was also the brother of the famous commodore. Regardless of its origin, the city's permanent name—Dallas—appeared in deed records in Aug. 1842.

DALLAS GROWS AND BECOMES CENTRAL TO THE REGION, 1850

The number of white settlers in Dallas grew to 2,356, the slave population was 207, and the area continued to grow. Many pioneers who settled in Dallas were farmers from Kentucky and Tennessee whose love for good, hearty soil permitted them to continue farming, even in the new region. The beginnings of industry, however, were starting to take shape. Local business was booming, led by Alexander and Sarah Cockrell, who together raised livestock and ran a freight business.

A CITY FOR SALE

In 1852, Alexander Cockrell bought Bryan's remaining acreage and his ferry license for $7,000. Cockrell immediately erected a toll bridge across the Trinity River, making transportation of people and goods easier and making him a rich man in the process. He then built a sawmill and a general store. Cockrell was gunned down in 1858 before the completion of his new hotel. He was murdered by the town marshal, who, unsurprisingly, owed him money.

After his death, Cockrell's widow continued his entrepreneurial enthusiasm and built a flour mill and finished the hotel.

LA REUNION

Victor Considerant, a visiting Frenchman looking to create a utopian community, La Reunion, in the Dallas area, returned to France to write "Au Texas," an essay encouraging his fellow Europeans to emigrate with him. In 1855, Considerant and 200 French, Swiss, and Belgians arrived in Texas. This group would be the first of many to hail from Europe and settle in the region. La Reunion, however, disintegrated in 1857, and its colonists moved to Dallas. The new residents brought diverse skills, knowledge, and cultural refinement never before found in the town.

WHEAT FOR SALE

At the close of the decade, the population was flourishing at a whopping 8,665 people, but with boomtown growth came boomtown complaints. Full granaries filled by the labors of local farmers lacked outside markets. The local economy was boosted when freight companies passed through and loaded up on local flour. Eventually, stagecoach service was added to Shreveport and other destinations. While significantly better, it was still a slow and expensive method of delivering saleable goods. The locals knew what was needed—a railroad.

The Houston & Texas Central rail company acquired the charter and plans to build a northbound line from Galveston Bay to the Red River that separated Texas from Oklahoma and would run a path from the very southern tip to the northern border.

The Social and Political Air Sours

FIRES, WHIPPINGS, AND HANGINGS, 1860

The wheat growers required fewer slaves than their cotton-farming counterparts, although the *Herald*, the town's weekly newspaper, was clearly pro-slavery and wielded a large influence over its readership. Stories about slave insurrections abounded, and residents grew suspicious. Anxieties peaked when a sudden fire erupted in the local drugstore, and 25 buildings were burned beyond repair. Locals learned of similar fires in other Texas towns, and vigilante committees were formed. After nearly a hundred slaves were interrogated, three were identified as the ringleaders and were hanged. All other slaves were whipped, and the two Iowa preachers believed to have coordinated the attack were jailed, whipped, and run out of town.

SUCCESSFUL SECESSION

Between the burning of the city and the election of Abraham Lincoln to the White House, dissent intensified. A resolution was unanimously adopted, declaring that Dallas County would not be governed by President Lincoln. On Feb. 23, 1861, Dallas residents voted 741–237 to secede from the Union, and the Civil War began June 8 of the same year.

WAR IS HELL

Local residents immediately rallied in support of the war, and provisions were cheerily donated to the southern war effort. While Dallas never saw fighting, the supply shortage that eventually came with the war effort did not spare the city. The economy shrunk, and prices for basic goods, when available, skyrocketed. Money was scarce, and wheat dropped severely in price.

From 1862 to 1864, Dallas became one of several quartermaster and commissary posts in Texas for the Trans-Mississippi Army of the Confederacy, enabling the city to survive economically until the end of the war.

THE RECONSTRUCTION AND THE WAR OVER RACISM AND FREEDOM WAGES ON

On June 19, 1865, Texan slaves were finally freed, two and a half years after Lincoln's Emancipation Proclamation. Many former slaves moved to the Metroplex, as it did not require rebuilding. Despite its economic difficulties, the area had remained one of the most prosperous Southern towns.

The Ku Klux Klan first appeared in 1868.

In Texas, Juneteenth is an official state holiday that celebrates the day news of the emancipation reached Texan slaves. Festivities organized by civic groups are celebrated in Texas cities each year on June 19.

The boom years

GREASED PALMS
AND RAILROAD BUILDING, 1872

After the Civil War, the Houston & Texas Central Railroad resumed construction, and its closest path was planned 8 miles east. Disappointed, town leaders met with railroad officials. The rail line owners asked for free right-of-way for their tracks, 115 acres of free depot acreage, and $5,000 cash—an extraordinarily large and greedy request. The voters overwhelmingly approved the measure, nonetheless, and the rail line was built.

Anxiety about reconstruction policies focused on the recently built Freedman's Bureau. Lt. William H. Horton, the bureau's only agent, arrested violators, but the courts refused to convict whites arrested for acts of violence against African Americans. Horton fought back and established his own mini-court. His opponents sued for false imprisonment, and Horton was eventually replaced with another agent. Horton's successor was murdered, and the next replacement stayed in the southern part of the county and rarely ventured into Dallas.

Citizens were already excited about the exponential growth brought by the railroad when they learned about the prospects of another railroad coming. Adding a crossroads of the Texas & Pacific railroad to the existing Houston & Texas Central line would ensure continued economic prosperity. The rail line owner requested the same deal, along with an additional $100,000 in bonds. Again, Dallas voters approved the measure. The city became a major distribution point for raw goods between the East and the frontier West and was a place for westward travelers to stock up on supplies.

THE NEW PLACE TO BE

Land values near the railroad skyrocketed, and the city became an attractive destination for eastern and northern businesses and manufacturers looking to expand. The economy diversified, and plenty of single men looking for work settled into the area; with those single men, however, came gambling halls, brothels, saloons, pickpockets, drunks, burglars, and an array of con artists.

The infrastructure struggled to keep up. Despite the town's resistance to raise taxes and build schools to meet the demand, learning did occur, and literacy levels rose. With literacy came reading, and Dallas became a new publishing hot spot. The Galveston newspaper sent a young George Bannerman Dealey to locate an area for a sister newspaper operation, and the *Dallas Morning News*, which still operates today, was born. The first issue was printed in October 1885.

In 1886, two competing fairs, the Dallas State Fair & Exposition and the Texas State Fair, opened. The fairs combined at a site in East Dallas the following year.

NEW CENTURY AND NEW GROWTH

Herbert Marcus, Carrie Marcus Neiman, and her brother Albert L. Neiman opened Neiman Marcus in 1907.

Dallas became the site of one of 12 regional Federal Reserve Banks in 1914. The city campaigned for years, and the bank's arrival assured Dallas's place as a financial center.

Southern Methodist University opened in 1915.

Frustrated by their dead-end retail jobs, the Neimans and Mr. Marcus moved to Atlanta in 1905 to begin a successful advertising business. They were offered a buyout of the agency, with an option for either $25,000 in cash or a Missouri-based franchise for an unknown beverage called Coca-Cola. The three opted for the money, much to their later dismay, though it did fund their first store in downtown Dallas, selling the finest women's clothing to the nouveau riche oilmen. The new store was immediately profitable.

Love Field was established as an aviation training ground during World War I.

Dallas led the world in cotton gin manufacturing in 1918.

The Majestic Theater, which still operates today, was completed in 1921—it was the first of the Elm Street vaudeville and movie palaces. The Magnolia Building, now a hotel, is completed.

Insider tip: Limited tours of the Dallas Federal Reserve Bank are available on Tues. and Thurs. at 10 AM and 2 PM, and requests must be made online three weeks on advance at www.dallasfed.org.

SOCIAL CHANGE IN BABY STEPS

Newspaperman G. B. Dealey and others worked to defeat the political and social influence of the Ku Klux Klan in 1923.

The State Fair of Texas created Negro Achievement Day in 1923, the only day during the three-week event that African Americans could attend. This day was scheduled annually until 1967.

Outlaws Find Their Way In

The infamous Belle Starr, the sharpshooter subject of many dimestore novels, worked initially as a singer and dancer in a Dallas dance hall, and then operated a livery where she sold stolen horses and harbored outlaws. John Henry "Doc" Holliday came to Dallas to restore his health and even opened a dental office with John Seegar. Holliday grew tired of his profession and turned his energy toward playing cards. He was an intense, quarrelsome gambler, and in 1875, he and the local saloon owner traded gunshots. Charges were eventually dropped, but Holliday was still run out of town.

Sam Bass, disappointed with the cowboy life in nearby Denton, became a train robber. He and his posse stole $60,000 in new $20 gold pieces, $1,300 in cash, and four gold watches from passengers from a single but lucrative robbery in the spring of 1878. They went on to rob another four Texas-area trains. Three months later, Bass was killed in an ambush near Round Rock by the Texas Rangers, a volunteer militia unit.

Texas Rangers lined up on horseback holding rifles, no date. Courtesy, Fort Worth *Star-Telegram* Collection, Special Collections, The University of Texas at Arlington Library, Arlington, Texas

NEW INDUSTRY IDEAS IN THE AIR

The City of Dallas purchased Love Field for $167,000 as a municipal airport in 1926. Passenger service to San Antonio and Houston began, transporting three or four passengers on a single flight.

PROGRESS THAT IS AS SLICK AS OIL

In 1930, oil was struck near Henderson, Texas, about 100 miles east of Dallas. The discovery strengthened the local economy, as 28 oil-related companies were created to support the burgeoning industry. Although Dallas was not fully spared the pains of the Great Depression, the oil discovery lessened its damage. Haroldson L. Hunt later purchased the Henderson-based company.

In 1934, the Flying Red Horse was installed on the Magnolia Building in honor of the convention of the American Petroleum Institute.

DALLAS GOES NATIONAL

The bodies of the infamous outlaw couple Bonnie Parker and Clyde Barrow, both native Texans, were delivered to Dallas after being gunned down in 1934 by Louisiana police.

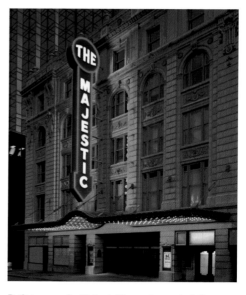

Built in 1921, the Majestic Theater is wonderfully restored with all of its charm and features sight-line seats, state-of-the-art stage/sound and lighting equipment. Performances include musicals from the Broadway Contemporary Series and Dallas Black Dance Theatre. Dallas CVB (Dallas Summer Musicals/Majestic Theater)

Big Tex being assembled in 1952. From the collections of the Texas/Dallas History and Archives Division, Dallas Public Library

Big Tex, the famous cowboy statue with a movable, waving arm that welcomes fairgoers, made his debut at the 1952 State Fair.

Insider tip: The iconic Flying Red Horse has since become the unofficial symbol of Dallas; look for it when traveling near downtown.

Big Tex, at 52 feet tall and made from papier-mâché, is so large that he wears size-70 boots and a 75-gallon hat and has fresh clothes made for him each year by local clothiers. Tex, however, did not start his life as a cowboy, but as a Santa Claus, and he was purchased from his original home in Kerens, Texas, for $750 after his novelty there wore off.

Insider tip: Both Bonnie and Clyde are buried in the Dallas area, and their gravesites are accessible to visitors. Parker is in Crown Hill Memorial Park, located at 9700 Webb Chapel Road in Dallas, and Barrow is in Western Heights Cemetery, located at 1617 Fort Worth Avenue in the Oak Cliff neighborhood in Dallas.

Neiman Marcus, by then a national chain, began its annual Christmas catalog in 1957, featuring outrageous gifts such as a $50,000 dirigible, a $7,000 ermine bathrobe, and a customized suit of armor for $20,000, sparking free publicity around the world.

Haroldson L. Hunt's son Lamar, perhaps with some financial help from his oil tycoon father, went on to start two professional sports teams in the city—the Dallas Cowboys football team and FC Dallas soccer team.

Bonnie and Clyde. From the collections of the Texas/Dallas History and Archives Division, Dallas Public Library

Thousands of onlookers came to see Bonnie and Clyde's still-bloody bodies and their getaway car. Their bodies and the car were nearly unrecognizable, as they were shredded by a spray of 167 bullets. Bonnie's corpse was still clutching her machine gun, and Clyde was still holding his revolver. After much public outrage from all over the country, their bodies were eventually buried in their respective burial plots.

CONSERVATIVISM IN BIG D
In the 1950s and 1960s, Dallas becomes ultraconservative politically, partly because of the national scare over communism.

THE ERA OF PROFESSIONAL SPORTS BEGINS
The Dallas Cowboys professional football team was born in January 1960, immediately after the creation of the American Football League by Lamar Hunt six months earlier. Originally labeled as the Rangers and brought in as an expansion team, the team eventually was renamed the Cowboys.

The story about a Neiman Marcus customer enjoying a chocolate chip cookie and then being sold the recipe is purely fictional, though it makes for a great tale. According to the legend, the waiter said that she could buy the recipe for "two-fifty," and the shopper agreed, believing the amount to be $2.50. She was shocked to receive her credit card statement the next month, only to find that she was charged $250, instead. Her alleged revenge was that she photocopied and distributed for free the recipe, thereby preventing the store from profiting further. Despite these falsehoods, the company did publish two subsequent cookie recipes to quell the rumors.

Both of Hunt's teams, the Cowboys and The Texans (his National Football League team) shared the Cotton Bowl in Dallas for three seasons. The Dallas Texans moved to Missouri and was transformed into the Kansas City Chiefs, leaving the Cowboys to remain in the

Each year, the owners of the Cowboys and the Chiefs battle for the Preston Road Trophy. The trophy is actually a plaque with a green street sign reading "Preston Rd.," and it was aptly named after the street where both Lamar Hunt, former owner, and Jerry Jones, current owner, had their offices. The trophy is held by the owner of the team that won the most recent Cowboys/Chiefs game until the next game. Both the Hunt and Jones families have continued the tradition, even after Lamar Hunt's death in 2006.

Cotton Bowl and to take over as Texas's only pro football team.

President John F. Kennedy was assassinated in downtown Dallas on Nov. 22, 1963.

Lamar Hunt founded the Dallas Tornado in 1967, one of the first soccer teams in the nation, which eventually becomes the Dallas Burn and then FC Dallas.

The Dallas Cowboys moved from the Cotton Bowl in Fair Park into their own Texas Stadium in 1971. Strangely, the Dallas Cowboys' then-new stadium was located not in Dallas but in nearby Irving (and even today, their stadium lies in Arlington, not Dallas).

The Dallas Cowboys holds the record for eight Super Bowl appearances and is the only team in the NFL with 20 consecutive winning seasons, from 1966 to 1985.

Several incidents painted the town, on a national level, as a haven for right-wing fanatics. One was a group spitting on and taunting Lyndon and Lady Bird Johnson, who were visiting during a campaign; a retired army general flew the American flag upside down over his concerns about communism taking over the nation to much public outrage; Ted Dealey, the successor and new publisher of the Dallas Morning News, lectured President Kennedy to be more aggressive; and Adlai Stevenson, after giving a speech, was struck over the head by a protestor's sign.

A National Tragedy in Downtown Dallas

With growing concern about his personal safety, President and Mrs. Kennedy arrived in the fervently conservative town for a visit. Despite the political tension of the times and even anti-Democrat rhetoric circulating in both the local newspaper and in local handbills, he and his motorcade were greeted by a cheering crowd that lined both sides of the street. In the front seat of his convertible were the driver, Governor Connally, and his wife Nellie Connally, and in the backseat were the president and Mrs. Kennedy. Mrs. Connally turned around to the President and said reassuringly, "Mr. President, you can't say Dallas doesn't love you."

As the motorcade turned onto Elm Street and entered Dealey Plaza through the applause and clicking cameras, several gunshots were fired. Both President Kennedy and Governor Connally were hit and immediately whisked away to nearby Parkland Hospital, where President Kennedy was pronounced dead from his wounds at 1 PM. Immediately after the announcement of the president's death, vice-president Lyndon B. Johnson was sworn in as president aboard Air Force One at Dallas's Love Field.

Former marine and Soviet Union defector Lee Harvey Oswald, suspected of firing his rifle at the president from the sixth floor of Texas School Book Depository building, was arrested an hour later at the Texas Theatre in the nearby Dallas suburb of Oak Cliff. Theories over the possibility of a second shooter abounded, and this shooter, if existed, was believed to be standing on the grassy knoll, a nearby hill just to the right of the depository. Oswald was questioned throughout the weekend about his Marxist sympathies and pro–Fidel Castro activities, and plans were made for him to be transferred from city to county facilities two days later. Television news crews who were filming the handover live captured on air another twist to the already unimaginable event—local nightclub owner Jack Ruby, who also had organized crime connections, shot Oswald in the basement of the Dallas Police Department, killing him. Ruby died of lung cancer in 1967 before his second scheduled homicide trial.

President and Mrs. Kennedy following their arrival on Air Force One at Love Field on November 22, 1963. © Bob Jackson

Insider tip: Lee Harvey Oswald is buried at Rose Hill Memorial Burial Park, located at 7301 East Lancaster Avenue in Fort Worth. His gravesite, which bears nothing more than a simple, placard-style headstone with his last name, is on the western edge of the park. Look for the curb markings denoting Sunset 18. The road forks near a mausoleum; take the path that nears the homes. Oswald's grave is about 20 feet from the cemetery road and located next to a grave marked Nick Beef. The original headstone, which had his full name and dates of birth and death, has long since been replaced with a simple, obscuring one. The cemetery staff, though polite, will not help visitors find the gravesite for fear of vandalism or harm.

The Dallas Tornado was part of Hunt's own United Soccer Association, which later became the North American Soccer League. Hunt, an avid sports fan and already a founder of the expansion teams that became the Dallas Cowboys and Kansas City Chiefs football teams, attended a World Cup match in 1966 in the United Kingdom and was inspired to bring professional soccer to the United States.

The Dallas Cowboys won the first of five Super Bowl victories in 1972.

After years of lobbying the American League for a baseball team, The Washington Senators were moved from Washington, D.C., to Arlington, Texas, in 1972 and were renamed the Texas Rangers.

FROM CITY TO METROPLEX

More than 600 companies, including Texas Instruments and Mary Kay Cosmetics Inc., are headquartered in the Metroplex, and the opening of Dallas/Fort Worth International Airport encouraged continued corporate growth. The airport opened in 1974 as the world's largest airport as a joint venture between the cities of Dallas and Fort Worth.

Forbes Magazine described the Cowboys as being the wealthiest team in the NFL, generating almost $269 million in annual revenue.

April 2, 1978—CBS debuted a five-part miniseries called *Dallas*, which was so successful it was transformed into a regular series. The show was shot entirely at Southfork Ranch in nearby Parker, Texas, but budget issues forced later productions to be shot partially in Hollywood (interior shots) and partially in Texas (exterior shots), until 1989 when the show was filmed entirely in California.

Millionaire Donald J. Carter and founding president and general manager Norm Sonju began to lobby the NBA for a Dallas-based basketball team. The league owners voted, and permission was granted, with the franchise entry fee of $12 million, in 1979.

Dallas was dubbed into 67 languages for 90 countries, and was one of the first television series to be distributed around the world. The show ended in 1991, but Southfork Ranch, about 24 miles northeast of the city, remains open to visitors (see recreation chapter for more information).

Prior to 1980, Dallas was home to the Chaparrals, a member of the American Basketball Association. In the Chaparrals' final game in Mar. 1973, they played the Carolina Cougars to a quiet crowd of 134 people. The following year, the Chaparrals became the San Antonio Spurs, and for the next seven years, Dallas did not have a basketball team.

DALLAS: A COCKTAIL OF SPORTS AND POLITICS

Dallas hosted the Republican National Convention at Reunion Arena in 1984, when the incumbents Ronald Reagan and George H. W. Bush were renominated for president and vice president, respectively.

Oil prices in Texas plummeted in 1986, and the local economy suffered significant financial losses.

Forty-one-year-old pitcher Nolan Ryan signed with the Rangers as a free agent in 1988.

Insider tip: When attending a Rangers game, get seats anywhere between home plate and first base. Your back will be against the sun, and this side is the first to get shade.

A group of investors led by Edward W. Rose and George W. Bush, who eventually became the 43rd President of the United States, bought a controlling interest in the Rangers in 1989.

In 1989, The Sixth Floor Museum, located in the infamous Texas School Book Depository building opened for the city to sort through and mitigate the stigma from its

The Reading Room inside the Sixth Floor Museum in Dallas. Architect's Rendering, Corgan Associates, Inc.

role in the assassination of President Kennedy.

Ann Richards, democratic governor of Texas, was defeated in 1994 by Republican and future President George W. Bush, who took over the gubernatorial office in 1995. The victory began his foray into American politics.

The Texas State Library and Archives in Austin, Texas, which is accessible online, houses the official records of George W. Bush's years as governor of Texas.

In 1995, Dallas investors buy the Minnesota North Stars hockey team, and the new Dallas Stars team is immediately successful.

The Dallas Burn wins its first championship—the Lamar Hunt U.S. Open Cup—in 1997.

The Dallas Stars win the Stanley Cup championship in the 1998–1999 season.

George W. Bush was declared President of the United States after a close election and a slew of questionable ballots from Florida in 2000 to a fiery national controversy and tense nation.

President George W. Bush moved from the White House to his new home in Dallas in 2009. Located in the north Dallas neighborhood of Preston Hollow, the residence is an 8,500-square-foot ranch house located in a tree-lined cul-de-sac and is inaccessible to onlookers.

Former Texas Rangers pitcher Nolan Ryan, hired as team president two years prior, purchased the Texas Rangers in early 2010 and led them to the World Series, for the first time in franchise history, in October of the same year.

Where the West Begins: Fort Worth

To establish control over the frontier, the Texas Rangers were established. When they proved inadequate, the United States Army stepped in and took over. It decided to create a barrier line of forts along the frontier west, one every hundred miles or so, stretching from the Rio Grande in the south to the Red River in the north.

In 1849, Major Ripley Arnold established a post on an expanse where the Clear and West forks of the Trinity River merged. With the aid of 42 men from Company F, 2nd Dragoons, Arnold built a fort on a high bluff; the fort had a clear view for miles in all directions.

Settlers joined them in the soil-rich area and were dependent upon the garrison economically and for their safety. The fort was built to keep peace between the native peoples and the settlers and to ensure that neither trespassed on the other's territory. Indian raids continued, however, in distant parts of Tarrant County.

Fort Worth was named in honor of the late Major General William Jenkins Worth, a hero of the Mexican-American War who died in a cholera outbreak.

Orders were given to close the fort, and on September 17, 1853, the troops were moved westward, establishing a new frontier line. Residents quickly transformed the vacated buildings into schools, churches, and even private residences. The town became a stagecoach stop for mail delivery, and the city barely survived.

THE EFFECTS OF WAR

The Civil War began in 1861, and many Fort Worth residents resisted enlistment. Nonetheless, Fort Worth became a recruitment center for the county's communities and served, more importantly, as a supplier of flour, corn, beef, leather, and even sewn uniforms out of locally grown cotton.

The population of Fort Worth shrank, partly because of absent soldiers, partly because of Unionists who left, and partly because of people fleeing eastward and out of reach of the frontier tribes. In 1864, inflation spiked, food shortages occurred, and slaves outnumbered the white population. With the town already weakened, nearby Comanche and Kiowa tribes raided Tarrant County. Fort Worth often went unscathed, thanks to the outlying settlements that buffered it.

1865, Fort Worth's role in the war as a provisioner led to economic stagnation afterward, and the one industry that ensured the town's survival was the need for meat. Northerners had an insatiable appetite for beef, and ranchers in Fort Worth and elsewhere in Texas were happy to provide it, though they had difficulty getting it to market.

> **Insider tip:** The Tarrant County Courthouse in downtown Fort Worth is a working museum today and a Texas Historic Landmark on the National Register of Historic Places. The native red granite building was built in Renaissance Revival style and has been known to make an occasional appearance on the TV series *Walker, Texas Ranger*.

MEAT: MEETING THE DEMAND

Starting in 1866, long cattle drives to Missouri and Kansas fed the demand for Texas beef. Several trails led north to the cattle-hauling railroads, and the legendary Chisholm Trail through Fort Worth was one of them. The trail took from six to eight weeks of hard riding; Fort Worth not only provided cattle but also became a supplier for the traveling cowboys and their herds.

The herds were a welcome sight for the Fort Worth residents, but the cowboys were known to cause trouble. The drinking and fighting led to the establishment of a red-light district in the south end of town, known as Hell's Half Acre.

The local Ku Klux Klan chapter held its first rally in 1868. Despite the presence of the Klan, it was not unusual to see black cowboys come through with the cattle

> Hell's Half Acre activities continued for years until the city used the land to build its Convention Center in the 1960s.

Purity Journal March 1906—page: Devil overlooking drawing of Fort Worth's Hell's Half Acre "Fort Worth: A Modern Sodom." Courtesy, Berachah Home Collection, Special Collections, The University of Texas at Arlington Library, Arlington, Texas

drives. Communities of former slaves began to settle in southern Fort Worth, to much local dismay.

In the early 1870s, the buffalo trade provided another revenue stream, but it ended sharply in 1876 after many of the herds were decimated.

Congress granted the first charter to The Texas & Pacific to build a transcontinental rail line along the 32nd parallel, driving through both Fort Worth and Dallas in 1871.

Insider tip: Cattle drives still occur each day on East Exchange Street in the Stockyards Historic District (see recreation chapter for more information).

PANTHERVILLE SLUMPS

The Panic of 1873 erupted, and as was the case for Dallas, the economic bubble burst in Fort Worth. The railroad construction halted midway between Dallas and Fort Worth, and the city's population plummeted.

Texas Wesleyan College, once named Polytechnic College, opened in 1881.

THE RAILROAD ROLLS INTO TOWN

The Missouri, Kansas & Texas Railroad arrived in 1881, followed by the Gulf, Colorado & Santa Fe Railroad the same year. The Cotton Belt railroad came in 1887, the Fort Worth & Denver City Railroad was built in 1888, and the Rock Island Railroad came into being in 1893, making Fort Worth a railroad hub. The city prospered again and was designated as a mail service headquarters.

More than 5 million cattle and one million mustangs, the greatest migration of livestock in the world, continued along the Chisholm Trail until an 1885 quarantine law was passed by Kansas, and a barbed wire fence closed off the trail permanently.

Fort Worth went from a Chisholm Trail stop to a railroad destination. Cattle pens were built to house the incoming cattle, and the city became the shipping point for beef and other livestock. The railroads saved the town, and Fort Worth became Cowtown.

Investors from all over the country bought property and diversified the economy. The year 1884, however, changed all of that when overexpansion, drought, and a glutted eastern beef market battered the local economy. Prominent citizens and companies both lost thousands of dollars, and tensions rose.

Baseball came to Fort Worth in 1887. The Fort Worth Panthers eventually became the minor-league Cats.

Although Fort Worth residents knew that this economic slump was temporary, they faced a battle against time. Congress assisted the building of the railroad but mandated that it be completed by the close of the 1876 legislative session on July 20th. Growing frantic, the town extended its city limits to meet the line, and the residents turned out en masse to finish the track themselves. Texas & Pacific's Engine No. 20 pulled into town one day before the Congressional deadline to much fanfare.

A Fort Worth resident pointed to some street markings and claimed, "That's where a panther slept last night." Nobody had seen a panther, but a young lawyer wrote a humorous letter to the newspaper, joking about Fort Worth's shrunken population and announcing that the town was so deserted that a panther slept unnoticed in the street. The nicknames Pantherville and Panther City stuck, much to the locals' amusement. A panther fountain was built in Hyde Park and 9th streets to commemorate the musings, and visitors can see it today.

The Saloon Shootout in Fort Worth

Hanging on the wall at the White Elephant Saloon in the Stockyards are two tombstone rubbings of famous gunslingers—Timothy I. "Long Hair Jim" Courtright and Luke Short. Versions of this story vary, but this seems to be the most colorful one, as provided by the City of Fort Worth.

Courtright, an established local, had a wide reputation for handling a gun and was known for his "border shift" maneuver. He would draw his pistol, fire it, toss the gun into his other hand, and then quickly resume fire—a showy but nonetheless impressive feat.

Generally, Courtright was well respected as the former city marshal and head of a detective agency, and he easily convinced the local establishments, particularly the saloons and gambling halls, that they needed his protection. All of them, that is, except Luke Short, the owner of the White Elephant Saloon, who also had a reputation for gunplay. He was also deemed to be an unscrupulous gambler with quick hands at the poker table.

On Feb. 8, 1887, the men had exchanged terse words outside Short's saloon, and both went for their guns. Short had fired the first bullet and hit Coutright's right thumb. Courtright had tossed his gun to "shift" it, but while it was still in midair, Short fired another three times, killing Courtright immediately.

Courtright was buried, and local law officials eventually ruled that the fight had been fair. Nonetheless, Short sold the saloon and moved to Kansas, where he died six years later of illness. Short's body was returned to Fort Worth and was buried, ironically, just a few feet from that of his former enemy, Jim Courtright. The gunfight is reenacted every February 8 for visitors to the saloon (for more information on the White Elephant Saloon, see nightlife listings in chapter 6).

Outlaws often preyed on Texas stagecoaches and trains, including the notorious Sam Bass and his gang. In an early Nebraska raid, Bass and his men stole $60,000 and four gold watches, and they moved their antics into Texas. In the spring of 1878, Bass robbed four trains in North Texas and was chased by the Texas Rangers, momentarily eluding them only to be killed shortly thereafter on his own 27th birthday.

LIVESTOCK LIVES LARGE

The first Fat Stock Show, now known as the Fort Worth Stock Show and Rodeo, was held in 1896. Ranchers used the show to promote their stock to the meat packers and to improve the local livestock industry.

Armour & Company and the Swift & Company meatpacking companies relocated to Fort Worth, and the city entered the meatpacking business in 1903. The plants competed, leading Fort Worth to become the meatpacking center of the southwest. An immigration wave brought thousands of Mexicans and Europeans to Fort Worth, seeking plant jobs.

The growing numbers of Hispanics caused anger in the white community, even though the meatpacking plants only hired Hispanics because they did not have enough white labor. Thirteen hundred people worked in the plants at any one time, and another 200 worked in the yards and Exchange building, where cattle business was conducted.

A NEW CENTURY INTRODUCES MODERN LIFE

The Fort Worth Cats won the league championship in 1904.

The Fort Worth *Telegram* newspaper purchased the struggling *Star* newspaper for $100,000 with the help of newspaper ad salesman and future oil tycoon Amon G. Carter, and the two companies merged in 1909 to create the Fort Worth *Star-Telegram*, the city's newspaper.

Insider tip: Deteriorated remnants of the Armour and Swift buildings, closed 1962 and 1971, respectively, can still be seen today in the Stockyards. They are fenced off, but occasional rumors circulate about returning these buildings to their original glory, perhaps as museums.

Texas Christian University opened in 1910.

The Canadian government selected Fort Worth as a training ground for the Royal Canadian Flying Corps. From 1915 to 1917, 3,000 pilots in all trained for the Western Front.

NEW INDUSTRIES

AND A MODERN WAY OF LIVING

1917—The oil and aviation industries came to Fort Worth, taking over as the city's primary industry. Oil was struck in outlying cities, even as far as West Texas, but Fort Worth was the nearest metropolitan town to all of the activity.

Insider tip: The Fort Worth Cats also won an unprecedented six consecutive championships from 1920 to 1925, and they still play today in their LaGrave Field home off Main Street, near the Stockyards.

Camp Bowie (pronounced Boo-ey), a 1,410-acre parcel west of town, trained 25,224 members of the 36th Infantry Division in World War I. The last soldier left in 1920, and locals took over the abandoned facilities. The military's presence had brought growth to the city's lagging infrastructure and left an indelible mark on the city's business sense—a taste for the military aviation industry. The local aviation business grew.

In the 1920s, while the rest of the nation prospered, Fort Worth suffered from labor strife and civic unrest. Problems in the railroad and meatpacking industries led to layoffs, and unemployment skyrocketed. The only industry that was not penetrated by the turmoil was the oil industry.

The Fort Worth Cats won the 1924 Dixie Championship at LaGrave Field.

The Air Mail Act of 1925 was passed, and Texas Air Transport was created for interstate

airmail service. It also began flying passengers to Houston for $30 round-trip. In
1929, the company was purchased by New
York–based Aviation Corporation, which
consolidated it with other regional airlines, becoming American Airlines.

The Works Progress Administration
and Civil Works Administration, which
aided the local economy in the midst of
the Great Depression, began to build the

Insider tip: Buried in Greenwood
Cemetery on White Settlement Road are 11
members of the Royal Flying Corps and the
daughter of an enlisted man. At the gravesite
is also a monument, and the small parcel of
land that contains it all officially belongs to
the British government because of Canada's
commonwealth status.

Burkburnett oil field showing oil wells with wooden derricks, ca. early 1900s to 1920s. Courtesy, Fort Worth *Star-Telegram* Collection, Special Collections, The University of Texas at Arlington Library, Arlington, Texas

Botanic Gardens, Will Rogers Memorial Complex, and even a couple of local high schools in 1933.

The city celebrated Texas' statehood, and Casa Mañana theater house opened as part of the 1936 festivities.

The city's low spirits changed with the beginning of World War II; while the war was never celebrated, the city embraced the resulting economic boom.

Consolidated Vultee, a B-24 bomber factory, opened in 1942, and Congress authorized activating a neighboring air base where some 4,000 pilots and crew would train. The base, now known as the Naval Air Station Fort Worth Joint Reserve Base at Carswell, hosts airlift and fighter/attack units from the Navy, Marine Corps, and Air Force reserves, and the plant, now Lockheed Martin, produced B-36, B-58, F-111, F-16, and F-22 airplanes during the war, continuing through the Cold War and until modern time.

In 1918, the Fort Worth *Star-Telegram* reported that five of the nation's top companies were in Fort Worth and would soon be handling 80 percent of the crude oil produced in Texas. Fort Worth had benefited from the business end of the oil industry without having the mess of the oil rigs.

The sale and purchase of oil leases and drilling operations was something akin to gambling. Some of the most notable and influential oil tycoons were Sid W. Richardson, Amon G. Carter, and W. A. Moncrief.

FUN AND DISCOVERY

Six Flags Over Texas, a 212-acre amusement park in nearby Arlington, opened in 1961.

American Airlines moved its headquarters from New York City to Dallas–Fort Worth in 1979, making DFW its main U.S. hub.

Billy Bob's Texas, the Stockyard's venue self-proclaimed as the "world's largest honky-tonk" opened in 1981.

Texas Motor Speedway, just north of Fort Worth, opened in 1997 to world-class Formula One and NASCAR racing.

Near the Cowboys and Texas Rangers stadiums sits the Arlington Archosaur Site, where a 2008 excavation unearthed fossils from archosaurs and crocodiles believed to be from 145 to 65 million years ago.

Sources

American Airlines. History of AMR Corporation and American Airlines. http://www.aa.com/i18n/amrcorp/corporateInformation/facts/history.jsp.

Americredit Presents Heritage Trails. http://www.fortworthheritagetrails.com/.

City of Fort Worth. From a Cowtown to "Cowtown." http://www.fortworthgov.org/government/info/default.aspx?id=3252.

Cook, Patricia. Arlington Archosaur Site: Dinosaurs in the Dallas Metroplex. Associated Content. http://www.associatedcontent.com/article/2394418/arlington_archosaur_site_dinosaurs.html?cat=37.

Dallas Historical Society. Dallas History. http://www.dallashistory.org/history/dallas/dallas_history.htm.

Three students at the newly integrated City Park Elementary in Dallas; this image was picked up nationally by Associated Press wire service and appeared in the September 18, 1961 issue of Newsweek *magazine.*

American Airlines plane at Amon Carter Air Field with flight crew standing on tarmac beside sign "Service to Chicago, New York," 03/27/1956. Courtesy, W.D. Smith Commercial Photography Collection, Special Collections, The University of Texas at Arlington Library, Arlington, Texas

Durango, Texas. Lee Harvey Oswald Gravesite. http://www.durangotexas.com/eyeson texas/dallas/oswald.htm.

Federal Reserve Bank of Dallas. History of the Dallas Fed. http://www.dallasfed.org/fed /dalhistory.cfm.

Find A Grave. Lee Harvey Oswald (1939-1963). http://www.findagrave.com/cgi-bin/fg .cgi?page=gr&GRid=781.

Fort Worth Stock Show and Rodeo. History and Tradition. http://www.fwssr.com/?page_id=212.

Georgia Humanities Council & University of Georgia Press. *The New Georgia Encyclopedia*: "John Henry "Doc" Holliday (1851-1887)." http://www.newgeorgiaencyclopedia .net/nge/Article.jsp?id=h-3001.

Hazel, Michael V., *Dallas*. Fred Rider Cotton Popular History Series. Center for Studies in Texas History at the University of Texas at Austin. Austin, TX: Texas State Historical Association. 1997.

Jennings, Diane. "Carrollton volunteers clean up old black cemetery for Juneteenth." *Dallas Morning News*, June 19, 2010.

Lone Star Publishing. *Celebrating Texas Lone Star Publishing: Honoring the Past, Building the Future*. Evanston, IL: McDougal Littell, 2003.

Main, Derek J., Welcome to the Arlington Archosaur Site. http://www.arlingtonarchosaur site.com.

Major League Soccer. The Legacy of Lamar Hunt. http://www.fcdallas.com/Legacy.

NBA Media Ventures, LLC. Mavs History. http://www.nba.com/mavericks/history /00400544.html.

Neiman Marcus Group. Investor Relations. http://phx.corporate-ir.net/phoenix
    .zhtml?c=118113&p=irol-overview.
NHL and Dallas Stars, L.P. Early Dallas Hockey History. http://stars.nhl.com/club/page
    .htm?bcid=sta_history.
PRLog. Dallas Cowboys vs. Kansas City Chiefs NFL live streaming online TV on PC.
    http://www.prlog.org/10371836-dallas-cowboys-vs-kansas-city-chiefs-nfl-live
    -streaming-online-tv-on-pc.html.
Selcer, Richard F. *Fort Worth : A Texas Original!* Fred Rider Cotton Popular History Series.
    Center for Studies in Texas History at the University of Texas at Austin. Austin, TX:
    Texas State Historical Association, 2004.
State Fair of Texas. Big Tex's History. http://www.bigtex.com/sft/AboutUs/BigTex.asp.
Texas State Historical Association. *The Handbook of Texas Online.* http://www.tshaonline.org
    /handbook/online.
Texas State Historical Association. *Texas Almanac: 2010-2011.* Denton, TX: The Texas State
    Historical Association.
Ultimate Dallas. "About the Show: Introduction to the TV Series Dallas." http://www
    .ultimatedallas.com/dallas.
White Elephant Saloon & Love Style Incorporated. Welcome to the Legendary White
    Elephant Saloon: The Historic Fort Worth Stockyards. http://www.whiteelephant
    saloon.com.

FORT WORTH
INTERMODAL TRANSPORTATION
CENTER

TRANSPORTATION

Here, There, and Everywhere

Given the enormous size of the Dallas–Fort Worth Metroplex, as well as its rich heritage in all aspects of the transportation industry, it is not surprising that there are plenty of transportation options for getting to and around DFW. Nonetheless, traveling the Metroplex can be difficult and requires advance planning. Visitors may encounter a large number of freeways and highways, many of which are complex, narrow, and congested at all times; another challenge is a lack of public transportation within most of the smaller communities and among them. The DFW area does not always have clearly marked signs along its roadways or freeways, either, so a map, a GPS, a GPS-enabled phone, or a sense of direction can be helpful, too.

GETTING TO DFW

By Air

Dallas Fort Worth International Airport (972-973-8888; www.dfwairport.com) 3200 East Airfield Drive, Dallas 75261. Located in the center of the Metroplex, the Dallas/Fort Worth International Airport (known by the airport code DFW) is, ironically, in neither Dallas nor Fort Worth but in Irving. DFW serves 59 million passengers yearly and 1,900 flights daily. The airport has five terminals, and each terminal has at least 40 gates. DFW is a major hub for American Airlines, American Eagle, and UPS Airlines, and it is the third busiest airport in the nation. All of these details translate into one warning: wear good shoes for walking. Navigating through the airport can be tricky despite its simple design.

To reduce walking time and help travelers get to their destinations, there is Skylink. It is a free high-speed train that connects to all five terminals, delivering connecting passengers to their new gates in about five minutes or less. There are two Skylink stations at each gate.

In additional to the usual shops and restaurants, DFW has several Wi-Fi providers buzzing throughout the airport. Most require short-term memberships or existing service relationships for free-rein connectivity, but there are also free data ports and power-

LEFT: *Fort Worth Intermodal Transportation Center.* Fort Worth Transportation Authority

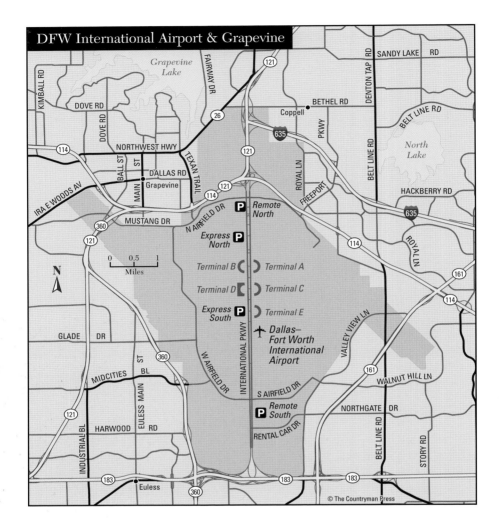

DFW International Airport & Grapevine

recharging kiosks for those who do not mind being tethered. The kiosks are available in each gate, but they have a limited number of terminals.

Free podcasts about DFW, its connecting flight information, and its parking options are available through iTunes in multiple languages. TripCase, another free application, delivers real-time flight information, gate changes, security wait times, and baggage claim information. Travelers can also retrieve their itineraries and send photos, and TripCase is available through the DFW website.

DFW is pet-friendly and has relief areas in each terminal. Most areas are beyond security checkpoints, so be prepared to be checked each time. Pets must be leashed at all times, and pet carriers must be kept handy. The airport also has an array of services including currency exchange, banks, and even portable DVD player/movie rentals at InMotion Entertainment. Upon your return, knowing which terminal and gate you need is vital to a stress-free trip back to the airport.

Dallas Love Field (214-670-6073; www.dallas-lovefield.com) 8008 Cedar Springs Road, LB 16, Dallas 75235. Love Field is an alternative to the hustle of DFW. It has only two terminals and is served by five airlines—Southwest, Continental, Delta, American Airlines, and American Eagle. Southwest considers Love Field its home base, and good prices and plentiful travel options may be available through Southwest and this facility.

Insider tip: Have plenty of coins on you at all times, even while driving in the airport. It isn't unusual for someone to get lost in and around the facility and to have to pay an entrance/exiting toll when looping around to get back on track.

Love Field is near downtown Dallas, and travelers should be patient in traffic when headed to and from the airport. Tune your radio to Love Radio 1580 AM for up-to-the-minute travel information.

By Car

The key to getting in and out of Dallas–Fort Worth, or at least on the main highways, is to think of a wishbone. On three out of four sides leading into the DFW area, the freeways leading into the Metroplex split and then miles later merge into one again.

Traveling north and south is I-35. They diverge when nearing the Metroplex, and two paths are aptly named I-35E (or east, which runs through downtown Dallas) and I-35W (or west, which runs through downtown Fort Worth), but yet are north- and southbound routes. Miles after passing through their respective downtowns, either north or south, these freeways merge again into one I-35.

Every major city within the mainland United States can be accessed within four hours of DFW Airport.

The DFW International Airport is so large that the U.S. Postal Service issued the airport its own zip code—75621.

Dallas/Fort Worth International Airport. Grapevine CVB

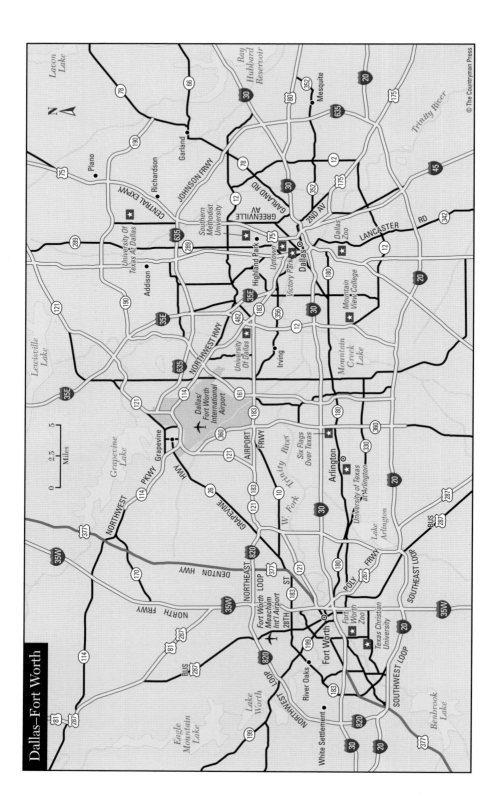

Dallas–Fort Worth

© The Countryman Press

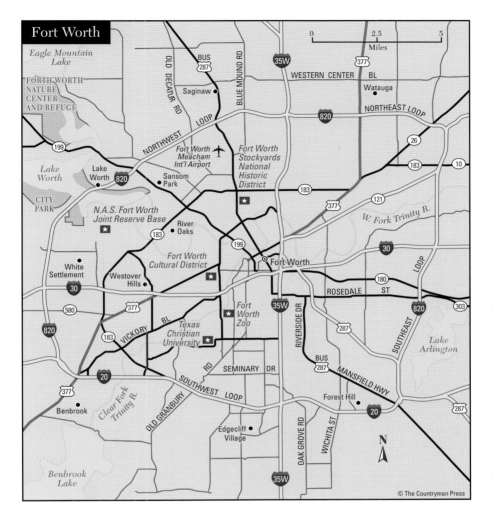

Fort Worth

From the west, leading into Fort Worth is I-20. Like its I-35 counterpart, I-20 splits into two. This time, however, the most northern route of the two becomes I-30 and still runs east/west. I-30 will take drivers near downtown of both Fort Worth and Dallas and is the most direct roadway between the two cities. Drivers coming from the east will want to take I-30 on the reverse of the path described above.

The other fork on the I-20 split maintains the I-20 name and is the southern route that also runs east/west. This path crosses through the far southern portions of Fort Worth, Arlington, Grand Prairie, and Duncanville and does not connect to the downtowns of neither Fort Worth nor Dallas, and as a result, usually has less traffic.

From the northeast is U.S. Highway 75, also known as the North Central Expressway, and it leads into Plano and downtown Dallas. This path is slow-moving and heavy with traffic.

Coming from the northwest is U.S. Highway 287, but it eventually hooks into I-35W southbound and leads into downtown Fort Worth.

By Train

Amtrak (214-741-7825; www.amtrak.com) Union Station, 400 South Houston Street, Dallas 75202, and **Intermodal Transportation Center** (817-332-2931) 1001 Jones Street, Fort Worth 76102. Amtrak's Texas Eagle route, which is a 41-city journey between Chicago and Los Angeles, stops in DFW. The rail company offers coaches, sleeper cars, and dining cars. Originating in Chicago, the train stops in Dallas and then Fort Worth and then travels onward. From the other direction, the stops are in reverse.

An offshoot route from the Texas Eagle that runs between Kansas City and Fort Worth, called the Heartland Flyer, stops in Tulsa, Oklahoma City, and Norman, which is convenient for Oklahoma-area travelers to get to Texas.

By Bus

Greyhound Lines, Inc. (1-800-231-2222; www.greyhound.com) Dallas Greyhound Station, 205 South Lamar Street, Dallas 75202, and **Intermodal Transportation Center** (817-429-3089) 1001 Jones Street, Fort Worth 76102. Taking a Greyhound bus is a cheaper method of travel, and it is certainly a viable way to travel to DFW. With two main stations in Dallas and Fort Worth and several small stops throughout the Metroplex, Greyhound may be one of the most direct methods of getting to your destination, wherever it may be. The smaller locales are:

Arlington Greyhound Station, 817-461-5337
Carrollton/Busy Bee, 972-242-3133
Dallas South Park and Ride, 972-228-8982
Dallas Westmoreland, 214-337-0010
Denton Travel Station, 940-387-3802
Fort Worth Greyhound Station, 817-429-3089
Fort Worth McCart, 817-920-1446
Mesquite Greyhound Station, 972-288-1374
Midway McKinney, 972-548-0647

By Private Airplane or Chartered Plane

There are at least 30 private and municipal airports throughout the Metroplex that serve private pilots and chartered aircraft. Prior arrangements are advised. Some of the airports are:

Addison Airport, 972-392-4850
Arlington Municipal Airport, 817-459-5570
Bridgeport Municipal Airport, 940-683-3996
Cleburne Municipal Airport Hazlewood Field, 817-641-5456
Collin County Regional, 972-562-4214
Commerce Municipal Airport, 903-886-1101
Dallas Executive Airport, 214-670-7612
Decatur Municipal Airport, 940-627-2855
Denton Airport, 940-349-7736
Ennis Municipal Airport, 972-875-1234
Fort Worth Alliance Airport, 1-800-318-9268
Fort Worth Meacham International Airport, 817-392-5400
Fort Worth Spinks Airport, 817-392-5400
Gainesville Municipal Airport, 940-668-4565

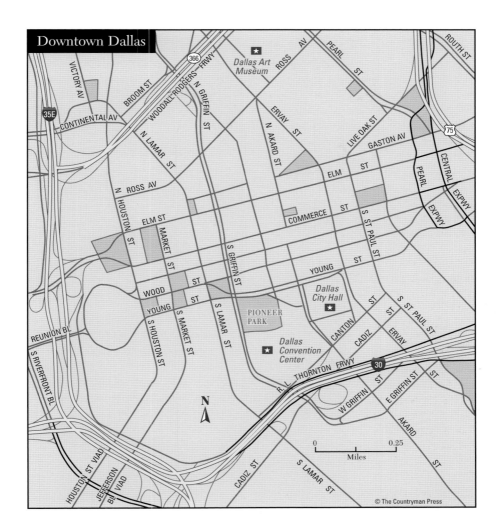

Downtown Dallas

Grand Prairie Municipal Airport, 972-237-7591
Greenville Municipal Majors Field, 903-457-2960
Lancaster Regional Airport, 972-227-5721
Mesquite Metro Airport, 972-288-7711
Mid-Way Regional Airport, 972-923-0080
Mineral Wells Airport, 940-328-7808
Rockwall Municipal, 972-771-0151
Terrell Municipal Airport, 972-524-1601

By Helicopter
Dallas Heliport (214-670-4338; www.dallascityhall.com/aviation/dallas_heliport.html)
801 South Lamar, Dallas 75202. The Dallas Convention Center has a dual-deck
heliport/vertiport, 65 feet in the air, available for public use. This facility, owned and
operated by the city, can accommodate three helicopters and two vertical-takeoff and

landing vehicles simultaneously. It also has a dedicated parking lot and a full-service lobby, a conference room, and a pilot waiting area for corporate visitors or private charters.

It is open 7 AM–10 PM daily, and prior arrangements are recommended. Contact its business office for overnight aircraft parking, ground transportation arrangements, or to reserve its conference room. Although the heliport is connected to the Dallas Convention Center, it cannot be accessed by the center but through the gate on the ground level.

Insider tip: If the idea of a helicopter ride is intriguing but you lack finds to buy your own helicopter, visitors can go on private sightseeing or aerial surveying tours through D/FW Heli-Tours at 972-723-5364 or visit www.dfw helitours.com.

Insider tip: Garland, a town just 13 miles north of Dallas, also has a heliport that is available for public use. Tours of downtown Dallas are available through Sky Helicopters, the heliport's fixed-based operator at 214-349-7000 or www.skyhelicopters.com.

GETTING AROUND DFW

Taxi Cabs

Taxi service is available at both airports and at most of the major hotel lobbies around the Metroplex. At DFW airport, taxi stands are located on the upper level of terminals A, B, C, and E and on the lower level of terminal D. The stands are open between 8 AM and midnight, and attendants are available to help arrange transportation. Riders can request a taxi between midnight and 8 AM at 972-574-5878. At Love Field, taxis can be obtained on the upper level across from baggage claim in the main terminal building. Some of the taxi companies include:

Alamo Cab Company, 214-688-1999
Ambassador Cab, 214-905-1111
Checker Cab, 972-222-2000
Cowboy Cab Company, 214-428-0202
Diamond Taxi, 214-349-3333
Eagle Cab Company, 214-421-7788
Executive Taxi, Inc., 972-554-1212
Freedom Cab, 214-712-0800
Golden Cab Company, 972-554-1212
Jet Taxi Inc., 1-800-538-8294
Ranger Taxi Company, 214-428-0202
Star Cab, 214-252-0055
State Taxi Cab Company, 214-630-9595
Taxi Dallas, 972-554-1212
Texas Cab Company, 214-599-9483
United Cab Services, 817-819-7787
Yellow Cab Company, 214-426-6262

By Courtesy Car and Shuttle Service

There are a variety of courtesy cars and shuttles that serve the DFW and Love Field airports, as well as select destinations throughout the Metroplex. At DFW airport, passengers

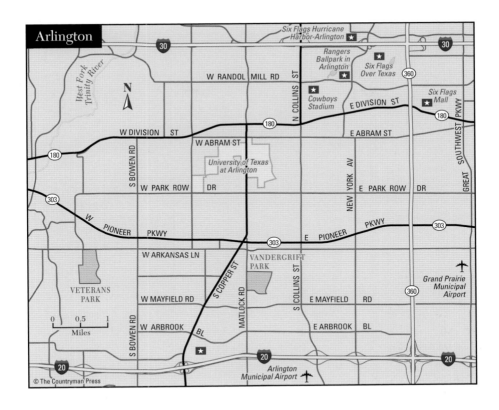

Arlington

board on the lower level of each terminal. Some services from the airport to various hotels are free, but travelers would be wise to inquire first.

There are also paid shuttle services that are ideal for transporting larger groups to and from the airport from most hotels and other locales. These shuttles are also available as a charter to various locations throughout the Metroplex. Yellow Checker Shuttle, for example, has 24/7 convention center shuttles and even Cowboys game-day shuttles. These services are ideal for travelers who plan to remain in one general area throughout their stay and are inclined to take other forms of public transit for neighborhood travel.

SHUTTLES
ACE, 214-352-4555
City Shuttle, 214-760-1998
Super Shuttle, 1-800-258-3826
Yellow Checker Shuttle (a.k.a Airporter), 972-222-2000 or 214-841-1900

COURTESY CARS
Many area hotels offer courtesy cars for guests. Check with your hotel when making reservations.

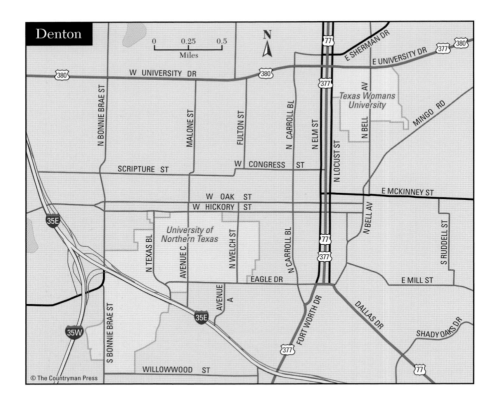

By Limousine

Limousine rentals are plentiful, and the costs can, in some cases, be comparable to taxi fare. A five-page list of recommended limo companies can be found at the DFW airport website at http://www.dfwairport.com/dfwucm1prd/groups/public/documents/webasset /p1_006652.pdf

Rental Cars

Rental Car Center 2424 East 38th Street, DFW Airport 75261. Car rental companies are conveniently located at both airports. The Rental Car Center at DFW is separate from the airport and located near the south entrance, and it is serviced by shuttles that pick up and deliver passengers in both directions every 10 minutes. Incoming guests should follow the Rental Car Center signs on the lower terminal to the designated pickup area, and returning guests can expect a shuttle ride from the car rental facility directly to the terminal. At Love Field, the rental car area is located directly at the airport. Some of the car rental companies are:

ACE, 214-352-4555 (only at Love Field)
Advantage Rent A Car, 1-800-777-5500 (only at DFW)
Alamo, 1-800-327-9633
Avis, 972-574-4130 or 1-800-331-1212
Budget, 1-800-527-0700

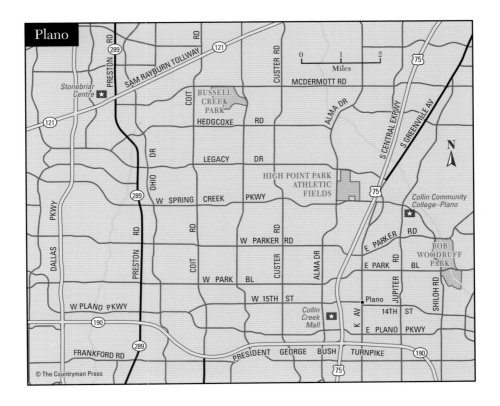

Plano

Dollar, 1-866-434-2226
Enterprise, 972-586-100
E-Z Rent-A-Car, 972-574-3360
Hertz, 972-453-4759
  or 1-800-654-3131
National, 972-615-5400
  or 1-800-227-3876
Thrifty, 972-456-5980

Insider tip: Call 1-866-MY-TRAFC or visit www.traffic.com for up-to-date information on accidents and congestion, road construction, and weather conditions in the DFW area.

A NOTE ABOUT DRIVING IN DFW

If you plan on doing extensive traveling throughout DFW, you really do need a car. Having a car allows visitors the freedom to adventure to locales beyond bus or train stops, but driving also means dealing with traffic congestion and parking challenges. Drivers need three words to survive driving in DFW: patience, patience, and patience. Here are a few practical tips that will help you keep your sanity:

There are turnarounds on many freeway off-ramps. These are, in essence, U-turn ramps in the far-left turn lane of an off ramp. They have one-way traffic and are intended to bypass traffic lights, alleviating left-turn-lane backups. These U-turns pass under the freeway, and drivers must yield to oncoming traffic. They allow for easy access to businesses or homes on the other side or for returning to the freeway after a wrong turn.

Along many frontage roads are left-side, one-lane on-ramps for quick and easy access to the freeway without much fanfare or signage. They are easy to miss for drivers who do not know what to look for and are usually independent of a stoplight. In complex areas, there can be more than one left-lane on-ramp to multiple nearby freeways.

Some freeway off-ramps are left exiting, and drivers need to watch for signs. These off-ramps can transition from one freeway to another or simply to surface streets. For that matter, some freeways actually fork off into multiple directions and can even change names without notice, so make sure to have a map handy.

There are several toll roads throughout Dallas County. Drivers should carry coins, currency, or even credit cards with them. Tolls range from $.22 to $2.15, depending on location. If you plan on doing a lot of driving, Toll Tags can be purchased through AAA or most major grocery stores and can save you money on fares.

Parking downtown can be challenging and expensive. Expect to pay up to $20 for parking. For special events and sports arenas, parking typically costs between $10 and $15; Cowboys Stadium parking can cost as much as $75.

During inclement weather, freeway bridges can be covered in black ice. Be careful!

By Rail, Bus, and Trolley

RAIL

Trinity Railway Express (214-979-1111; www.trinityrailwayexpress.org) 1600 East Lancaster, Fort Worth 76102. The Trinity Railway Express (TRE) is a commuter rail service

The TRE and bus system working together. Fort Worth Transportation Authority

that links downtown Fort Worth, downtown Dallas, and DFW airport. It origi-
nates out of Fort Worth's Texas and Pacific
Station and ends at Dallas's Union Station
and takes approximately one hour from
one to the other. The TRE can provide
hassle-free traveling on the 35-mile
stretch between the two cities and compa-

Insider tip: If you board the TRE without a valid ticket and are caught, you may be issued a $75 citation. Do not take unnecessary chances!

rable to driving in a car in terms of time, given heavy traffic and unpredictable roadways.

Regular rail service is provided Mon. through Sat. from 5 AM–11:45 PM and 7:19 AM–11:45 PM on Sun. There is no holiday service, and schedules are modified for the eves of major holidays. Forty-nine trains run daily, and additional trains may be scheduled for special events.

Passengers may board the TRE at several stations including Union Station, Victory Station, Medical/Market Center, South Irving, West Irving, CentrePort/DFW, Hurst/Bell, Richland Hills, Intermodal Transportation Center, and Texas and Pacific Station. Passengers who ride the TRE to the DFW airport can ride the shuttle from the CentrePort/DFW Airport station bus stop to the remote south parking lot and transfer to their choice of terminal shuttles.

Travel along the TRE is broken into two zones, and the DFW airport, which is considered the final stop in the first zone on the Fort Worth side, is also the dividing line between them. For a single ride, from either side of this division in only one zone, fare is $2.50, and for both zones, fare is $3.75. Day passes are either $5 or $7.50, for one- or two-zone travel, and weekly passes are $25 and $37.50, respectively. Ticket dispensers are at each station, and riders should arrive 15 minutes prior to their scheduled departure.

Single-ride tickets are good for transfer to the T, the local bus service in Fort Worth. Single-ride tickets are also good for train-to-train transfers from TRE to DART and are valid for 90 minutes.

BY BUS

Dallas Area Transit (214-979-1111; www.DART.org) 1401 Pacific Avenue, Dallas 75266. Taking the Dallas Area Rapid Transit (DART) is one travel option for downtown Dallas, as well as the greater Dallas area. DART is a bus and rail transit service that serves Dallas and 12 of its neighboring communities including Addison, Carrollton, Cockrell Hill, Farmers Branch, Garland, Glenn Heights, Highland Park, Irving, Plano, Richardson,

Insider tip: Travel on DART and the TRE is easy except on the day of the University of Texas vs. Oklahoma University football game at the Cotton Bowl stadium. This game occurs in Fair Park during the annual State Fair in October, and buses and trains are notoriously overcrowded and delayed.

Rowlett, and University Park. These routes serve high-interest locales such as the American Airlines Center, DFW Airport, Love Field Airport, Dallas Museum of Art, Dallas World Aquarium, Sixth Floor Museum, Reunion Tower, the Meyerson Symphony Center, the West Village, the Dallas Medical/Market Center, the Magnolia and Majestic Theaters, the Federal Reserve Bank of Dallas, and hotels.

DART offers several levels of transit that determine fares. A local fare is any ride on the red, blue, and green line trains and local busses. System fares include all DART buses and trains, use of the Trinity Railway Express (train with endpoints in Dallas and Fort Worth) but only between Union Station and West Irving Station, and DART on-call (personalized, shared van service) and FLEX service (hybrid of fixed-route local bus service and off-route curbside service). Regional fares include all DART busses and trains (except paratransit), all Trinity Railway Express service (includes the T in Fort Worth), DART on-call, and FLEX service. Paratransit services are personalized door-to-door services for riders with disabilities unable to utilize traditional fixed-route buses or trains. Vanpools, which accommodate 8 to 15 passengers, are also available to groups, and costs can vary.

Single-ride fares range from $1.75 (local destination) to $2.50 (system destination) to $3.75 (regional destination). Day passes, which provide unlimited rides for the day, are valid until 3 AM the next morning and range from $4 (local) to $5 (system) to $7.50 (regional). Weekly passes are also sold at $20 (local), $25 (system), and $37.50 (regional). Exact fares are required. Routes are subject to change, and it is best to check the website or call.

Tickets can be purchased at most Albertsons, Fiesta stores, and Minyard Food Stores, as well as online and at station kiosks. The DART stations in downtown Garland, Glenn Heights, South Irving, Westmoreland, and the Parker Road and Bush Turnpike areas also have parking lots.

THE T BUS SERVICE

Fort Worth Transportation Authority (817-215-8600; www.the-t.com) 1600 East Lancaster Avenue, Fort Worth 76102. The T is the Fort Worth bus service that covers the city and extends, in a few routes, beyond. Downtown routes, served by red, white, and blue buses, are free and make it easy for travelers to visit many of the popular locales including the DFW airport. All regular fares are $1.50 one-way. Tickets for the T can be purchased online through the Fort Worth Transportation Authority or at local Carnival Food Stores, Sack 'n Save, and Fiesta Food Stores. Routes are available on weekends and are subject to change.

BY TROLLEY

Arlington Trolley (817-504-9744; www.arlingtontrolley.com) P.O. Box 941, Arlington 76004. The Arlington Trolley makes stops at various locations through Arlington's entertainment district, including Six Flags Over Texas, Six Flags Hurricane Harbor, Texas Rangers Ballpark, Cowboys Stadium, Arlington Convention Center, and Arlington Visitor Information Center. It is free and runs every half hour, though riders must be staying at one of 23 select hotels. Riders must be 13 years of age and older, and all riders must be able to present a key as proof of hotel stay.

M-Line Streetcar (214-855-0006; www.mata.org) 3153 Oak Grove Avenue, Dallas 75204. Finally, something for free! The M-Line Streetcars, à la vintage trolley cars, allow visitors to ride up and down historic McKinney Avenue for free. The M-Line cars, with updated interiors and air conditioning, operate daily 7 AM–10 AM, Mon. through Thurs., 7 AM–midnight on Fri., and 10 AM–midnight on Sat. and connect to the west entrance of Cityplace Station on the DART Rail system for extended travel.

Nearby attractions include the Dallas Museum of Art, Southern Methodist University, the West End, the West Village, the Angelika Film Center and Café, The Magnolia Theatre, the original Neiman Marcus, NorthPark Center mall, and a range of shops and hotels.

Service, however, is not limited to nearby places; the ride can be an experience unto itself. The M-Line's Dine-A-Round is an exciting chance for visitors to travel along McKinney Avenue and then stop to sample the cuisine in three first-class restaurants in the neighborhood. Prices for Dine-A-Rounds are about $90 per person, but both the restaurant choices and costs can vary with each dining experience. Starting at the Cityplace Station, the trolley stops at its first restaurant for an appetizer, a second stop for the main course, a third stop for dessert, and then a final loop around to its origination site. Thirty-two riders are needed to fill the trolley, and reservations are taken through PayPal. Charters are also available, and the M-Line hosts birthday parties, sit-down dinners, business meetings, and even weddings in the cars themselves.

Molly the Trolley (817-215-8600; www.mollythetrolley.com) Molly is a vintage trolley system that provides quick and easy travel to popular spots in Fort Worth. There are three routes: the Downtown Get Around, Stockyards Shuttle, and Sundance Lunch Line.

The Downtown Get Around is free and runs daily, every 15 minutes 10 AM–10 PM. It stops at Sundance Square and a variety of downtown hotels and passes by interesting places like the Fort Worth Convention Center, Bass Performance Hall, and Fort Worth Water Gardens.

Insider tip: For routes and times, text "Molly" to 38714 or call 817-215-8600.

The Stockyards Shuttle is $1.50 one-way and runs between downtown Fort Worth and the Stockyards. Available on Saturdays only from 9 AM–10:30 PM, it stops at several downtown hotels, as well as the Fort Worth Stock Exchange and the Intermodal Transportation Center.

The Sundance Lunch Line is also free and runs every 10 minutes. Available Monday through Friday from 11 AM–2 PM, it is a fast way to travel between Sundance Square and the west end of downtown Fort Worth. Stops are at Tarrant County College/Radio Shack, Chesapeake Energy, BBVA Compass/Whitley Penn, and Burnett Plaza.

3

LODGING

Not Quite Home, But Better Than Being a Houseguest

The Dallas–Fort Worth Metroplex is large enough that whatever your preferred accommodations are, whether it's the grandness of a historic downtown hotel, the quaintness of a
bed-and-breakfast, or the standardization of a chain hotel, it's here. The Best Westerns,
Days Inns, and Radissons are perfectly fine, albeit commonplace. If you're looking for a
truly unique lodging experience, however, read on. These locales were selected because
they were unique, artsy, historic, or off the beaten path.

Most folks book their lodging accommodations online these days, via their favorite
travel-planning search engine like www.hotels.com, www.orbitz.com, www.travelocity
.com, www.expedia.com, www.priceline.com, www.hotwire.com, or www.kayak.com, with
new ones popping up every day. If you know in which part of the Metroplex you wish to
stay, you can find a more localized approach to searching for hotels online, through these
websites or by visiting that city's convention and visitors' bureau online. For Fort Worth,
visit www.fortworth.com/visitors/hotels; for Arlington, www.arlington.org/accommoda
tions; for Dallas, www.visitdallas.com; Denton, www.discoverdenton.com; Plano,
www.planocvb.com/main/accommodations.php.

Standard check-in time is 3 PM and checkout at noon, but some hotels may have different stipulations or can accommodate an
early check-in or late checkout, so be sure
to ask. Many hotels will also store your
baggage if you arrive too early to check in,
or conversely, fly out past the checkout
time, but don't want to drag your luggage
around all day. Also, most hotels do not
permit animals, but some will allow small
pets for a nominal fee; if you're traveling
with your pooch, call the hotel to make
sure your furry friend is welcome. If you
would prefer a smoking room, you may
have a hard time finding one, so be sure

Insider tip: As widespread as it is now,
don't assume you will have free Wi-Fi in your
room. Most hotels do offer free service in
public areas such as the lobby, but you may
have to pay for access from your room. If
you're planning to get some work done in-
room, you will want to verify the availability
prior to booking your room or better yet,
bring your own air card.

LEFT: *The Gaylord Texan Hotel and Lake Grapevine.* Grapevine CVB

to ask about the hotel's smoking policy before making a reservation (see our "Tobacco Consumption Laws" section in Chapter 9).

Please know we have chosen not to list rates for the properties listed, as they are always subject to change.

ARLINGTON

Blue Cypress Hotel (817-633-4000; www.bluecypresshotelarlingtontx.com) 117 South Watson Road, Arlington 76010. Located just minutes from Arlington's Entertainment District and sports stadiums, the Blue Cypress hotel recently underwent a full renovation, and a stay there now features free continental breakfast, free parking, an exercise facility, indoor and outdoor pools, in-room safes, Jacuzzi tubs, flat-panel TVs with cable in every room, Wi-Fi, coffeemakers, and microwaves. Transportation to and from the Cowboys Stadium is available.

Comfort Suites (817-460-8700; www .comfortsuites.com/hotel-arlington-texas -TXB38) 411 W. Road to Six Flags Drive, Arlington 76011. Think you know Comfort Suites? New in Arlington's entertainment district, this hotel is anything but run of the mill. Sleek and modern in its design and furnishings, it offers guests a free hot, full breakfast, and its spacious suites contain microwaves, mini-fridges, flat-screen plasma TVs with cable, and pillow-top mattresses, among the other hotel-room standard offerings. Other amenities include Wi-Fi, a 24-hour grab-and-go pantry, an outdoor pool, a picnic area with barbeque grills and playground equipment, a free *USA Today*, an on-site fitness center, laundry facilities, and free parking. Comfort Suites is pet-friendly, too. Located just a stone's throw away from Six Flags, Hurricane Harbor, Texas Rangers stadium, Dallas Cowboys stadium, Arlington Convention Center, and Lincoln Square for shopping, dining, and salons, and only about 10 minutes from DFW airport.

Crowne Plaza Suites (1-877-270-1393; www.ichotelsgroup.com) 700 Avenue H East, Arlington 76011. This all-suite hotel is conveniently and centrally located right between Dallas and Fort Worth and only 8 miles from DFW Airport. Minutes away from Six Flags, Hurricane Harbor, Texas Rangers stadium, Dallas Cowboys stadium, Arlington Convention Center, and Lincoln Square for shopping, dining, salons, and more, the Crowne Plaza Suites has amenities that include concierge services, a 24-hour fitness center, an indoor heated pool, a sauna, a whirlpool, a full-service restaurant, a complimentary airport shuttle, free Wi-Fi, a 24-hour business center, and a sleep package that includes eye masks, drape clips, and lavender mist. On-site laundry facilities and safety deposit boxes are available at the front desk.

The Sanford House Inn and Spa (817-861-2129; www.thesanfordhouse.com) 506 North Center Street, Arlington 76011. The Sanford House Inn and Spa is a luxurious boutique hotel located in historic downtown Arlington. It has just 12 rooms, which include four one-bedroom cottage suites; two two-bedroom and two-bathroom villas; and six spacious manor house rooms, all with private bathrooms. A full breakfast is included, and homemade cookies and juice are customary upon arrival. The executive chef creates and directs all dining menus for breakfast and lunch served daily and fine dining every Fri. and Sat. night. The Van Gogh Bar and Lounge offers a happy hour 4 PM–6 PM Thurs. and Fri. The award-winning in-house salon/spa is a stunning venue where both men and women can experience a vast selection of salon and spa services (Tues. through Sat.). Check their website for amenities, as they vary by room type; romantically themed packages are also available online.

DALLAS

The Adolphus (214-742-8200; www.hotel adolphus.com) 1321 Commerce Street, Dallas 75202. Opulent in its baroque splendor and refinement, The Adolphus is one of America's most legendary addresses—imperial and grand, with a rich sense of history. Amid regal Flemish tapestries and an ornately carved Victorian Steinway once owned by the Guggenheims, you can sense the aura of the famous guests who have preceded you—from Babe Ruth and the Vanderbilts to U2, Oscar de la Renta, Donald Trump, and Queen Elizabeth II.

Conveniently located in downtown Dallas, The Adolphus is in the heart of the financial district; steps from eclectic restaurants; a short drive to shopping at NorthPark Center mall; and blocks from the Sixth Floor Museum, Dealey Plaza, and the flagship Neiman Marcus. Amenities include dining at The French Room, which was rated "number one hotel restaurant in America" by Zagat; full-service concierge (call direct at 214-651-3540 for advance reservations for theater, symphony, opera, sports, and other tickets); valet parking (nightly fee); a 24-hour business center; boutique/gift shop; complimentary sedan transportation within a three-mile radius (schedule varies, based on occupancy and demand); private in-room dining, which can include special menus for restricted diets; a fitness center; and free Wi-Fi.

World-class cuisine and old world charm combine to create an unforgettable dining experience at the French Room in the Adolphus Hotel. Dallas CVB (Adolphus Hotel—Dallas)

Bailey's Uptown Inn (214-720-2258; www
.baileysuptowninn.com) 2505 Worthington
Street, Dallas 75204. This lovely B&B is
within walking distance of some of Dallas's
best restaurants and shops and less than a
block from the M-Line that serves Uptown
and downtown Dallas. Antique-filled
rooms come complete with a private bath, a
comfortable sitting area, Wi-Fi, and
DIRECTV. Nearby attractions include the
Sixth Floor Museum at Dealey Plaza, Dallas
World Aquarium, Dallas Museum of Art,
West Village (shopping and dining center),
Dallas Symphony Center, American
Airlines Center, and the Majestic Theater.
Three spas are within walking distance.
Continental breakfast is served during the
week at 8:30 AM, and a full breakfast is
served on weekends at 9:30 AM, including
fresh fruit, juice, coffee, tea, and one of the
innkeeper's specialties, like French toast
stuffed with cream cheese and strawberries
or a southwestern frittata. Bailey's also has
flexible check-in/checkout times.

Belmont Hotel (866-870-8010; www
.belmontdallas.com) 901 Fort Worth
Avenue, Dallas 75208. Rising high above
Oak Cliff on a landscaped stone bluff, this
funky boutique hotel is like entering a different city entirely, even though it's only 2
miles west of downtown Dallas. A far cry
from all things snobby, the Belmont is
known for its style, its swimming pool, and
its cocktail lounge, BarBelmont, which
boasts "the best drinks and views in the
city." Amenities include complimentary
self-parking (valet also available), Wi-Fi,
flat-panel TVs, a year-round outdoor pool,
a health club/fitness center, on-site
dining at SMOKE restaurant, and room
service. Know that the Oak Cliff neighborhood can seem to outsiders to be a little,
shall we say, sketchy, but don't be put off by
this—this hotel is top-notch. The hotel
says they will gladly drive you to the Bishop
Arts District or downtown if you lack
transportation.

The Belmont Hotel pool. Gisela Borghi-Hocker

The Glass Cactus lounge in Grapevine. Grapevine CVB

Gaylord Texan Hotel and Convention Center (817-778-2000, 1-866-782-7897; www.gaylordhotels.com/gaylord-texan) 1501 Gaylord Trail, Grapevine 76051. Within its 4.5 acres of indoor gardens and winding waterways, you'll discover fine dining and casual restaurants, unique boutiques, and a 25,000-square-foot day spa and fitness center. For late-night excitement, including live music and dancing, nothing can match the energy of Glass Cactus nightclub, a favorite of many locals as well as hotel guests. Every hotel room features Wi-Fi, in-room coffee service, refrigerators, a large bath area with double vanities and makeup mirrors, and an in-room safe that can even charge your laptop battery while you're away. Not that you have any reason to venture outside, but there is an outdoor pool as well. The hotel also offers 24-hour concierge service, car rentals, a business center, 24-hour room service, valet parking, and even 24-hour transportation services. Check the hotel's website for specials, upcoming events, and packages (including a Murder Mystery Dinner Theater weekend, Little Girls' Diva Party, Dallas Cowboys game-weekend specials, and sizzling romance packages).

Insider tip: The hotel charges self-parking fees, and depending on their capacity, it can be quite a walk to the hotel from the parking area. If you have a lot of luggage, drive all the way up and leave it with a bellman before parking or just surrender your vehicle to the valet.

Insider tip: Whether staying at the Gaylord Texan or not, do not miss ICE!, an indoor exhibit with a wonderland created entirely from 2 million pounds of ice, kept at a chilling 9 degrees (don't worry, they provide coats) from November to January. It's like walking into a snow globe; tickets are not cheap, but it's an amazing experience.

The Great Wolf Lodge in Grapevine. Grapevine CVB

Great Wolf Lodge (1-800-693-9653; www
.greatwolf.com/grapevine/waterpark) 100
Great Wolf Drive, Grapevine 76051. Base
camp for family fun, the rustically elegant
Great Wolf Lodge offers an array of suite
styles that comfortably sleep between four
and eight guests. Standard amenities
include granite countertops, mini-fridges,
coffeemaker, microwave, clothes drying
line, wet bar, and of course, your stay
includes passes to the indoor, year-round
water park. The hotel is also home to a full-
service spa, dining, shopping and an ice
cream–themed kid's spa, Scoops.

Magnolia Hotel (214-915-6500; 1-888-
915-1110; www.magnoliahoteldallas.com)
1401 Commerce Street, Dallas 75201. One
of the city's most recognizable buildings,
the Magnolia Hotel Dallas is upscale and
modern. Its famous Pegasus, or the Flying
Red Horse, is illuminated at night and
shines brightly as the icon of Dallas from
atop this beautiful boutique hotel. The
Magnolia Hotel is conveniently located near
the American Airlines Center, the Dallas
Convention Center, the Dallas Zoo, West
End, Deep Ellum, Dallas Museum of Art,
Dallas Arboretum, Dallas World Aquarium,
Fair Park and the Cotton Bowl, and the flagship Neiman Marcus. The hotel offers a
breakfast buffet; an evening reception featuring domestic beer and house wine (5:30
PM–6:30 PM); bedtime cookies-and-milk
buffet (8 PM–10 PM); downtown transporta-

There are technically "airport hotels" (and probably nice hotels) very close to Dallas Love Field airport as well, but the location is so dodgy, we recommend you go straight to your destination and stay
in that area. In a pinch, the Wingate by Wyndham at 8650 North Stemmons Freeway (I-35E), 214-
267-8400, www.wingatedallas.com is a nice choice near Love Field.

The historic Pegasus atop the Magnolia hotel in downtown Dallas. Courtesy of Malen Yantis Public Relations

tion to and from most major corporate headquarters (weekdays); Wi-Fi; room service; a club lounge with full bar, kitchen, and a billiards room; and 24-hour fitness room with Jacuzzi. Paid overnight valet parking or day parking is available.

The Stoneleigh Hotel & Spa (866-539-0036; www.stoneleighhotel.com) 2927 Maple Avenue, Dallas 75201. Following an extensive $36 million renovation, the Stoneleigh Hotel & Spa has been fully restored to its roaring 1920s art deco grandeur. Nestled in the heart of Dallas's posh Uptown neighborhood, this AAA four-diamond property is conveniently located near the American Airlines Center, Dallas Museum of Art, Nasher Sculpture Center, NorthPark Center mall, and several other art galleries, museums, restaurants, and shopping areas. Amenities include Wi-Fi, a full-service day spa, in-house luxury dining at Bolla, 24-hour concierge and room service,

> **Insider tip:** Parking in downtown Dallas is scarce, to say the least. If you need to park your car long-term (for more than 24 hours), know that the valet services at downtown hotels can be pricey, but it is the safest way to go, so be prepared to pay.

a fitness center, daily newspaper delivery, currency exchange, and nightly turndown service.

W Dallas—Victory (214-397-4100; www.whotels.com/dallas) 2440 Victory Park Lane, Dallas 75219. W Dallas—Victory defines the emerging it-spot in Victory Park as an upscale playground near downtown, Uptown, Turtle Creek, the high-style Design District, and the city's nightspots. Hang out at Ghostbar, de-stress at Bliss Spa, or take a dip in the 16th-floor infinity pool wrapped in a panoramic view of Dallas's famous skyline (cocktails and bites

> **Insider tip:** Book online under "specials and packages" for hotel-spa-dining package deals rather than booking that massage upon your arrival.

are available poolside from Wet). Standard amenities include pillow-top mattresses, down-filled pillows (hypoallergenic available upon request), goose-down comforters, 32-inch flat-screen TVs with Internet access, a video player, weekday newspaper delivery (upon request), a rain-forest shower, an alarm clock radio with iPod docking station, and 24-hour in-room dining. Pets are welcome.

The Westin Dallas/Fort Worth Airport
(972-929-4500; www.starwoodhotels.com
/westin) 4545 West John Carpenter Freeway, Irving 75063. Comfortable with quick
airport access—what more could you ask for
on a business trip? Rooms feature their
famous amenities the Heavenly Bed and the
Heavenly Shower/Bath. They also have a
data port, cordless phones, 24-hour room
service, a workout room, and an in-room
safe. The Westin is also pet-friendly.

FORT WORTH

The Ashton Hotel (817-332-0100; 1-866-
327-4866; www.theashtonhotel.com) 610
Main Street, Fort Worth 76102. The Ashton
Hotel, an AAA four-diamond property, is
an elegant boutique hotel fully renovated
from two buildings on the National Register
of Historical Places. The buildings were
meticulously restored to retain their unique
architectural details, while the interiors
were updated with the latest amenities. Its
39 spacious rooms and suites contain cus-
tom-designed furniture, designer linens,
and their signature Ashton king-size bed
dressed with down pillows. A separate large
bathroom, robes, in-room coffee, Wi-Fi,
iPod docking stations, and flat-screen tele-
visions are just a few of the deluxe, standard features. In-house refreshments
include afternoon tea or upscale dining at
SIX 10 Grille. The downtown location is
ideal for getting around the city and visiting
Fort Worth's most popular attractions—the
convention center, Sundance Square, the
Stockyards, and the museum district.

**The Azalea Plantation Bed & Breakfast
Inn** (817-838-5882; 1-800-687-3529;
www.azaleaplantation.com) 1400 Robin-
wood Drive, Fort Worth 76111. This stately
country inn, nestled near the heart of Fort
Worth, is refreshingly relaxing for being so
close to all the action. Enjoy the gardens
and gazebo, where you will likely be visited
by birds and squirrels. A full buffet is
served for breakfast daily from 9 AM–10 AM
in the elegant dining room, where tables
are set with fine linens, vintage china, and
stemware. In addition to breakfast, amenities include king-size beds; whirlpool tubs;
freshly baked cookies; complimentary bottled water, soft drinks, coffee, and tea;
robes and custom bath accessories; Wi-Fi
and cable TV; and a DVD, VCR, and CD
player in every room with complete access
to their library of books and music. In
addition to these standard features, the
cottages also contain a mini-fridge,
microwave, and coffeemaker. Within 10
minutes lies Sundance Square, where dining, shopping, and entertainment choices
abound—the Stockyards, Museum District,
Fort Worth Zoo, and Fort Worth Botanical
Gardens. You can call ahead to arrange
romantic "extras" for your visit.

The Texas White House Bed & Breakfast
(817-923-3597; 1-800-279-6491; www
.texaswhitehouse.com) 1417 Eighth Avenue,
Fort Worth 76104. This quaint B&B offers
five rooms, two of which are suites, complete with a fireplace, two-person
whirlpool tubs, and a sauna. Business
guests will appreciate being close to downtown Fort Worth and to the medical district.
Families will love the nearby Fort Worth
Zoo, Log Cabin Village, Trinity Park, Bass
Performance Hall, Omni Theater, Fort
Worth Water Gardens, and more. Romantic
couples will find fine restaurants within a
few minutes and relaxation in the backyard
gazebo and Texas Star Gardens.
Therapeutic, on-site massage services are
available and a full gourmet breakfast at a
time of your choosing begins each day.
Check the website for amenities offered
and to preview the decor of each of their
five rooms; specials are also offered online.

The Worthington Renaissance Fort Worth (817-870-1000; www.marriott.com/hotels/travel/dfwdt-the-worthington-renaissance-fort-worth-hotel/) 200 Main Street, Fort Worth 76102. Dubbed "The Star of Texas," with its western-themed, yet elegant decor, the Worthington is Fort Worth's original AAA four-diamond luxury hotel. Located downtown in historic Sundance Square, the Worthington is moments from the Stockyards, the Museum District, and Texas Christian University. Hotel amenities include an indoor pool and whirlpool, in-house dining at Vidalias Southern Cuisine, a fitness center, in-room coffee and tea, and newspaper delivery to rooms upon request. Know that the Worthington charges for parking and in-room Wi-Fi. Pets are allowed with a refundable deposit.

PLANO

Aloft Plano (214-474-2520; www.starwoodhotels.com/alofthotels) 6853 North Dallas Parkway, Plano 75024. Aloft features bold, loft-inspired design in the booming business center of Plano. Aloft Plano offers easy access to a long list of corporate quarters and is close to upscale retail, dining, and entertainment. Rooms are sleek, stylish, and include a 42-inch LCD flat-panel TV with cable, a walk-in shower with an oversize showerhead, Bliss Spa bath products, a mini-fridge, an in-room safe, and Wi-Fi. The hotel also offers shuttle service (within the surrounding area), parking, a pool table, and video and board games. There are also TVs in the lobby, a trendy lounge for socializing, an outdoor pool, 24/7 gym access, and a 12-and-under play area for kids. Before you pack it in for the night, head down to the wxyz bar for cocktails and munchies while you jam to live music or sassy DJ mixes.

4

Culture

The Spirit of a Community

Introduction

There's something about the culture of a community that reveals its inner greatness, and the Metroplex has it all—over 75 institutions of art, science, history, music, dance, gardens, and far more than can be listed here (but in the interest of squeezing in as many as possible, some are listings only, while others contain blurbs about their respective offerings). These institutions preserve, record, and not only bring alive the history and nature of the area but also represent an ever-expanding archive of knowledge for generations of visitors, locals and tourists alike, to learn and enjoy. We just hope you have your walking shoes, reading glasses, and cameras at the ready.

Please note that in addition to operating hours listed, most of these institutions are closed entirely on major holidays such as Thanksgiving Day, Christmas Eve, and Christmas Day.

Arlington

Arlington Museum of Art (817-275-4600; www.arlingtonmuseum.org) 201 West Main Street, Arlington 76010. Open: Wed. through Fri. 1 PM–5 PM, Sat. 10 AM–5 PM, Sun. 12 PM–5 PM. Admission: Free; donations welcome. See website or call ahead for current exhibits and upcoming events.

Levitt Pavilion for the Performing Arts (817-543-4301; www.levittpavilionarlington.org) 100 West Abram Street, Arlington 76010. Open: Always. See website or call ahead for upcoming performances, dates, times, and ticket pricing (usually free). In summer and fall, you can catch a show almost any night of the week—it could be rock, country, jazz, classical, Latin, world music, or even a comedy show at this beautiful outdoor amphitheater. Numerous outdoor festivals and weekend-long events are held at and around the Levitt as well, like Ecofest in September, organized by the City of Arlington to promote environmental awareness. Most shows are family-friendly, and refreshments are usually available on-site.

LEFT: *Bass Hall is a glorious venue for musicals or concerts.*   Forth Worth CVB

Symphony Arlington (817-385-0484; www.symphonyarlington.org) at Arlington Music Hall, 224 North Center Street, Arlington 76011. See website or call ahead for upcoming performances, dates, times, locations, and ticket pricing.

DALLAS

African American Museum (214-565-9026; www.aamdallas.org) 3536 Grand Ave, Dallas 75210. Open: Tues. through Fri. 11 AM—5 PM, Sat. 10 AM—5 PM. The African American Museum, located in Fair Park, is the only museum in the region dedicated to the preservation and display of African American artistic, cul-

> The Dallas Public Library is home to one of the original copies of The Declaration of Independence and William Shakespeare's *Comedies, Histories, and Tragedies*. Free of charge; seventh floor.

tural, and historical artifacts. The museum proudly features a small but authentic collection of African masks, sculptures, gold weights, and textiles, and its permanent collections include African art, African American fine art, and research library/archives documenting the accomplishments and history of the local African American community. The African American folk art collection, one of the largest in the nation, is housed in four vaulted galleries. Educational and entertainment programs take place in the facility's on-site theater and classrooms. The museum offers tours for groups of 10 or more and has a gift shop on the premises.

Cavanaugh Flight Museum (972-380-8800; www.cavanaughflightmuseum.com) 4572 Claire Chennault, Addison 75001. Open: Mon. through Sat. 9 AM—5 PM, Sun. 11 AM—5 PM. Admission: Adults $8, seniors and military $6, children 4—12 $4, children 3 and under free. Formal tours can be arranged by calling 972-380-8800, Mon. through Fri. 9 AM—5 PM. The Cavanaugh Flight Museum is known for two things: restoring, operating, maintaining, and displaying vintage aircraft and offering rides on most of its pieces. Visitors can enjoy the collection that documents the history of aviation on a self-guided basis by reading the informative signs near each aircraft or display; however, formal museum-guided tours are also available by appointment and are given by a knowledgeable crew of volunteers. The aircraft are spread throughout four large hangars, and visitors should plan on spending one or two hours viewing the exhibits. As some of the aircraft on display appear regularly at air shows throughout the country, the museum's roster of airplanes changes frequently, bringing in new and fresh items for visitors to see. The museum offers rides over north Dallas in two distinctive warbirds, the PT-13 Stearman and the AT-6 Texan, as well as a Stearman Biplane and a Bell 47 helicopter, as well as others. On-site is also a gallery of aviation art, often featuring dual signatures from the artist and the featured pilot of a particular aircraft. Special events are also held there, including book signings and lectures from notable people in American history. Consult the website for scheduled flights. There is a gift shop at the museum.

Cold War Air Museum (coldwarairmuseum.com) 850 Ferris Road, Lancaster 75146. Open: Sat. 10 AM—4 PM, and by appointment. Join us, comrades, at the Lancaster Air Base, a little Soviet air base located just south of Dallas at the Cold War Air Museum where a number of Soviet aircraft are on display and are flown. The museum is home to

The Cavanaugh Flight Museum in Addison. Monica Prochnow

flying aircraft, as well as related artifacts, artwork, political, and library resources highlight the history and culture of the period. A portion of the 45,000-square-foot museum is a working restoration facility committed to actively returning many Cold War–era aircraft to the air, and the Iron Curtain Air Force, which contains MiG-21UM Mongol B, MiG-23 Flogger, Antonov AN-2, Mil MI-24 Hind, and the AH-1 Cobra and UH-1 Huey helicopters.

Dallas Arboretum (214-515-6500; www .dallasarboretum.org) 8525 Garland Road, Dallas 75218. Open: Daily, 9 AM–5 PM. Admission: Adults (13–64) $10, seniors (65+) $9, children (3–12) $7, children 3 and under free; On-site self-parking $7.

Dallas Firefighters Museum (214-821-1500; www.dallasfiremuseum.com) 3801 Parry Avenue, Dallas 75226. Open: Wed. through Sat. 9 AM–4 PM. Admission: Adults $4, children $2. The Dallas Firefighters Museum, located across from the main

The vibrant colors of spring greet visitors at the Dallas Arboretum. The park, open year-round, features native trees and plants in beautifully manicured gardens. Dallas CVB/Courtesy of the Dallas Arboretum

Tranquility abounds in the beauty of the Dallas Arboretum. Dallas CVB/Courtesy of the Dallas Arboretum

entrance at Fair Park, is located in one of the city's oldest working fire stations. Built in 1907, the station was the home to Hook and Ladder Company No. 3 and boasts an impressive collection of old fire equipment, covering over 100 years. The museum's pride, Old Tige, an 1884 horse-drawn steam pumper, is a 600 GPM pumper that once served the downtown area until its retirement in 1921. Other exhibits include some of the first motorized engines that were also used by the Dallas Fire Department. Children are welcome to climb on a 1951 fire engine housed on-site, wear the helmets, and even pretend they are en route to a call. The collection of extinguishers, helmets, tools, and uniforms serves as a backdrop to the working fire station that takes calls, responds to alarms, and serves the community.

Dallas Holocaust Museum (214-741-7500; www.dallasholocaustmuseum.org) 211 North Record Street, Dallas 75201. Open: Mon. through Fri. 9:30 AM–5 PM, Sat. and Sun. 11 AM–5 PM. Admission: Adults $6, seniors (55+) $4, students (under 18) $4, active military $4, groups of 15 or more $4.

Dallas Museum of Art (214-922-1200; www.DallasMuseumofArt.org) 1717 North Harwood Street, Dallas 75201. Open: Tues. through Wed. 11 AM–5 PM, Thurs. 11 AM–9 PM, Fri.–Sun. 11 AM–5 PM. Admission: Adults $10, seniors (65+) $7, military personnel (with current ID) $7, children under 12 free. The Dallas Museum of Art is the heart of downtown Dallas's art district. The museum's collections contain more than 24,000 works of art spanning 7,000 years of human creativity. The museum is especially known for its arts of the ancient Americas, Africa, Indonesia, and South Asia; European and American painting, sculpture, and decorative arts; and American and international contemporary art. It also hosts a variety of programs to engage visitors of all ages and has eight to 10 special exhibits annually. Works from big-name artists and famous traveling exhibits often appear within these walls. A local favorite is its Late Night event on the third Friday of the month, when the museum remains open until midnight. Free live music is also featured every Thurs. from 6 PM–8 PM at its weekly Thursday Night Live! event. The museum also has a diverse spectrum of programs, from exhibitions and lectures to concerts, literary readings, and dramatic dance presentations. Strollers are welcome, but in busy times you might be asked to wait until more space is available. Diaper bags and frontal carriers are also welcome, but backpacks and other large bags are not permitted and can be left at the coat check located near the main entrance. Wi-Fi service is free. Bring your smart phone to access information on select works within the collections. There are two restaurants and a gift shop on the premises. Underground parking is available in the garage on a first-come, first-served basis for $10.

Dallas Opera (214-443-1000; www.dallasopera.org) Winspear Opera House, 2403 Flora Street, Dallas 75201. See website or call ahead for upcoming performances, dates, times, and ticket pricing.

Dallas Symphony Orchestra (214-692-0203; www.dallassymphony.com) Meyerson Symphony Center, 2301 Flora Street, Dallas 75201. See website or call ahead for upcoming performances, dates, times and ticket pricing.

Eisemann Center (972.744.4650; http://www.eisemanncenter.com)Eisemann Center for Performing Arts and Corporate Presentations, 2351 Performance Drive, Richardson 75082. Critical acclaim not only for events, but for the facility and its architectural design.

The Dallas Symphony Orchestra, under the direction of Jaap Van Zweden, performing at the Morton H. Myerson Symphony Center in Dallas. Dallas CVB (DSO)

Eisemann Center. Monica Prochnow

Frontiers of Flight Museum (214-350-3600; www.flightmuseum.com) 6911 Lemmon Avenue, Dallas 75209. Open: Mon. through Sat. 10 AM–5 PM, Sun. 1 PM–5 PM. Admission: Adults: $8, seniors (65+) $6, youth/students (3–17) $5, children under 3 free. Located near Love Field airport, the Frontiers of Flight museum chronicles the evolution of flight, starting with the Wright brothers, who tackled man's dream of flying, to aviators of the 1920s and 1930s, onward to the airplanes and the sacrifices of fliers during World War II, and ending at today's jet and rocket propulsion systems. The role played by the Dallas–Fort Worth area in the evolving aviation industry is prominently featured. The museum allows visitors to see, hear, and touch in a multisensory exhibit some of the local and rare artifacts that have been amassed here, including items from the now-defunct Braniff Airlines. Highlights include a World War I Sopwith "Pup" biplane, remnants of the famed dirigible the *Hindenburg*, an Apollo 7 Command Module, moon rocks, and exhibits honoring both the Royal Air Force's local No. 1 British Flying Training School based in nearby Terrell and the women of the 601st Women's Army Service Pilots, along with hundreds of models, uniforms, decorations, engines, and propellers. Guided tours are available between 10 AM and 4 PM Mon. through Sat. and 1 PM–4 PM on Sun. Reservations can be made online or over the phone.

Hall of State (214-421-4500; www.hallofstate.com) 3939 Grand Avenue, Dallas 75315. Library hours: Wed. through Fri. 1 PM–5 PM, by appointment only. Texas history is alive and in full grandeur at the Hall of State, which was built in 1936 as part of the State Fair's Texas Centennial Exposition. While most museums contain history, this one *is* history. On the exterior are two large pillars outside the double doorways made of Texas limestone that rise 76 feet to meet a field of blue mosaic tile. These serve as a backdrop to a statue of the Tejas Warrior, depicting one of the native people who lived on the Texas lands and for whom the state was named. The 11-foot-tall figure in bronze gilded with gold leaf appears to be shooting his arrow to the heavens. When they step closer to the front door, visitors may notice regal motifs on the front doors, symbolizing industry and agriculture of the state. The doors open up into the Hall of Heroes, which celebrates the early men who shaped the Republic of Texas. Farther above the door at the top of the building is a relief sculpture of a female figure that represents the State of Texas; she is kneeling behind a symbolic state flag, holding a glowing torch that represents Texans' fiery spirit. Nearby is an owl that represents wisdom and holds the key to progress and prosperity, resting on branches of the state's official pecan tree. Immediately through the double doors and inside is the Great Hall is a 12-foot gold medallion with a five-pointed star surrounded by six female figures, each representing the history of Texas under the flag of six nations: the Union, the Republic of Texas, the Confederacy, Mexico, France, and Spain. There are also two three-story-high murals depicting Texas history from the 1500s through 1936. Inside all this art deco beauty is the Dallas Historical Society, which appropriately is home to much of today's archived history of the area. Entry is to the Hall of State is free, and visitors are invited to see the local history that is featured here during its designated library times. The Hall of State has been the premier site for honoring presidents and other dignitaries who have visited Dallas, and it can also be rented for private functions.

Mary Kay Museum (972-687-5720; www.marykaymuseum.com) 16251 Dallas Parkway, Addison 75001. Open: Mon. through Fri. 9 AM–4:30 PM. Admission: Free. Tours are available, by appointment only, Mon. through Fri. at 10 AM and 2 PM. You can also schedule a free guided tour by appointment only of the Mary Kay manufacturing facility located at 1330 Regal Row in Dallas. The hours for manufacturing tours are: Mon. at 2 PM, Tues. through

Thurs. at 10:30 AM and 2 PM. The Mary Kay Restaurant is on the first floor of the Mary Kay Building. From grilled sandwiches to fresh salad or a choice of entrées, the restaurant offers a wide selection, including a sumptuous selection of gourmet desserts. Stop by the Mary Kay Restaurant for lunch between 11 AM and 1:30 PM, or drop in to enjoy coffee, a latte, or other refreshments and desserts until 3:30 PM.

> The number 13 was Mary Kay Ash's lucky number. The Company was founded on Friday, September 13, 1963. And the Mary Kay Building has 13 floors and 13 passenger elevators.

Museum of Nature & Science (214-428-5555; www.natureandscience.org) 1318 South Second Avenue, Dallas 75210. Open: Sun. 12 PM–6 PM, Mon. through Fri. 10 AM–5 PM, Sat. 10 AM–6 PM. Admission: Varies, based on general admission, IMAX admission, planetarium admission, or combined admission. Founded in 1936 during the Texas Centennial, the Museum of Nature & Science was one of the first natural history museums in the region and is the only public collections-based, research-driven natural history museum in the region. The museum is comprised of three gorgeous art deco–style buildings, and its "Nature" building houses more than 200,000 artifacts, eco-facts, entomology, vertebrate and invertebrate paleontology, malacology, ichthyology, herpetology, ornithology, and mammal specimens. The collections chronicle 1.7 billion years of Earth's history through exhibits on geology, earth sciences, biodiversity, a fossil-prep lab, and a live animal room. The "Science" building, the more interactive portion of the museum, contains 200 permanent hands-on exhibits in physics, astronomy, health, robotics, nature, and designated kids' areas, including a dinosaur dig, a heat-sensory exhibit, and a big nose that demonstrates sneezing every few minutes. On-site is also an IMAX theater with a 79-foot domed

Just one of many exhibits at the Museum of Nature and Science. Monica Prochnow

screen and 12,000 watts of surround and overhead sound that feature fun and interesting films. In the third building is the facility's planetarium, the only public one in the city.

Museum of the American Railroad (214-428-0101; www.dallasrailwaymuseum.com) 1105 Washington Street, Dallas 75204. Open: Wed. through Sun. 10 AM–5 PM. Admission: Adults $7, children 3–12 $3, children under 3 free. The Museum of the American Railroad in Fair Park possesses one of the most comprehensive heavyweight passenger car collections in the United States. Included are a complete, pre–World War II passenger train, a railway post office, a baggage car, coaches, lounge cars, Pullman sleeping cars, freight cars, and a dining car. The museum has more than 30 pieces of historic railroad equipment including steam, diesel, and electric locomotives; cabooses; historic structures; signals; and an assortment of small artifacts. The museum's highlights are the Big Boy, the largest steam locomotive ever built, and a Centennial, one of the largest diesel engine types ever made. The exhibits on-site display a rare sampling of steam, electric, and diesel-engine locomotives. Visitors can get on and off select trains and view displays of the interiors as they were in the 1940s. There is a gift shop on-site.

Insider tip: Travelers planning on visiting more than one museum at Fair Park can save money by purchasing a Fair Park Passport at a significant discount at any ticket office.

Nasher Sculpture Center (214-242-5100; www.nashersculpturecenter.org) 2001 Flora Street, Dallas 75201. Open: Tues. through Wed. and Fri. through Sun. 11 AM–4 PM, Thurs. 11 AM–8 PM. Admission: Adults $10, seniors (65+) $7, military with ID $7, students with ID $7, children 12 and under free; all admissions free on first Saturday of the month, 10 AM–5 PM.

National Scouting Museum (972-580-2100; www.bsamuseum.org) 1329 West Walnut Hill Lane, Irving 75038. Open: Mon. 10 am–7 pm, Tues. through Sat. 10 am–5 pm, Sun. 1 pm–5 pm. Admission: General $8, school groups $5, senior $6, children 4–12 $6, Scouts/Scouters $5, children under 4 free; all admissions free on Sun. and Mon.; free admission for all active military personnel/families from Memorial Day through Labor Day.

Old Red Museum of Dallas County (214-745-1100; www.oldred.org) 100 South Houston Street, Dallas 75202. Open: Daily, 9 AM–5 PM. Admission: General $8, seniors (65+) and students (with ID) $6, children 3–16 $5, children under 3 free; Sunday Early Bird Special $5 for tickets purchased before noon; groups of 20 or more $5 only with advance arrangements. The Old Red Museum, located in a bright red Romanesque courthouse built in 1892, chronicles the history of Dallas and its surrounding area from the early pioneering days to contemporary time. Included are exhibits that reflect Dallas's role in politics, industry, and even sports, on local and national levels. Old Red also doubles as a visitors' center, so make sure to stop by for additional details on the local scene.

Sixth Floor Museum at Dealey Plaza (214-747-6660; www.jfk.org) 411 Elm Street, Dallas 75202. Open: Mon. 12 PM–6 PM, Tues. through Sun. 10 AM–6 PM. Admission: Adults $13.50, seniors (Ages 65+) and youth (ages 6–18) $12.50, children 5 and under free. The Sixth Floor Museum at Dealey Plaza, located on the sixth and seventh floors of the famous Texas School Book Depository, was believed to be the location from which Lee Harvey Oswald shot President John F. Kennedy. This early 20th-century warehouse was transformed from

The National Scouting Museum in Irving. Irving CVB

a crime scene to a museum, helping people of all ages to find information about and understand the events that led up to the president's assassination on November 22, 1963. Museum tours are self-guided from an audio guide (included with admission). Narrated by Pierce Allman, the first reporter to broadcast from the Texas School Book Depository on November 22, 1963, the guide features discussions of the museum's permanent exhibits, as well as excerpts of historic radio broadcasts and recollections from the actual voices of reporters, police officers, and witnesses to the assassination. Audio guides are available in English, French, German, Italian, Japanese, Portuguese, and Spanish, and a youth version of the audio guide is available. The Dealey Plaza Cell Phone Walking Tour features a narrated guide and map of the neighborhood outside the museum, most notably the infamous grassy knoll. On-site is the museum's reading room, which provides researchers access to more than 4,000 books, magazines, newspapers, and videos that cover all aspects of President Kennedy's life and death. The museum also features a store and café.

Texas Discovery Gardens (214-428-7476; texasdiscoverygardens.org) 3601 Martin Luther King Junior Boulevard, Dallas 75210. Open: Daily, 10 AM–5 PM. Butterfly House Exhibit Admission: Adults $8, seniors $6, children $4. The Texas Discovery Gardens is a year-round organic urban oasis for visitors of all ages located in Fair Park. Visitors are invited to learn about butterflies, bugs, and botany in a gorgeous 7.5 acres of scenic landscape. Make sure to visit their new Rosine Smith Sammons Butterfly House and Insectarium, where you can stroll through the canopied walkway and surround yourself with hundreds of tropical butterflies and plants. The butterfly house is home to about 500 types of butterflies. Every day at noon, newly emerged butterflies are released, and visitors are welcome to watch as the handlers teach lessons on the importance of restoring, conserving, and preserving nature, even in urban environments. Lessons are taught with a focus on gardening organically and sustainably to maintain a high quality of life, which is why the gardens are the perfect home for the annual Dallas Green Festival that takes place every September.

There are also numerous family attractions such as the smart car rally, outdoor recreation zone, lifestyle demos, and recycled arts and crafts. Visitors are welcome to bring a picnic and dine on the outside picnic tables or sprawl out on their lawns. Guests are asked to be mindful of weddings that occur on the property.

The Trammell & Margaret Crow Collection of Asian Art (214-979-6430; www.crow collection.com) 2010 Flora Street, Dallas 75201. Open: Tues. through Thurs. 10 AM–9 PM, Fri. and Sat. 10 AM–6 PM. Admission: Free.

Women's Museum (214.915.0860; www.thewomensmuseum.org) 3800 Parry Avenue Dallas, 75226, Open Tues. through Sun. 12 PM–5 PM (Closed Mondays). Admission: Adults: $5.00; Senior Citizens and Students 13–18: $4.00; Students 5–12: $3.00; Under 5: Free.

DENTON

Denton County Historical Museum (940-380-0877) 5800 North Interstate 35, Denton 76207. The Denton County Historical Museum features a treasure of preserved history in the form of vintage photographs, maps, documents, and artifacts from days gone by. Exhibits from its permanent collection reveal the history of Denton County from early times until the 1950s, showing farm and ranch history, early schools, pioneer families, businesses, and the old-fashioned way of life. Relics include the collections of many pioneer families—family photographs, clothing, Bibles, newspaper clippings, and legal documents—and the museum has a reference library for researchers. The museum has a gift shop on-site.

FORT WORTH

Amon Carter Museum of American Art (817-738-1933; www.cartermuseum.org) 3501 Camp Bowie Boulevard, Fort Worth 76107. Open: Tues., Wed., Fri., Sat. 10 AM–5 PM, Thurs.

The Amon Carter museum. Fort Worth CVB

Women's Museum, Dallas

Bass Hall is a glorious venue for musicals or concerts. Fort Worth CVB

10 AM–8 PM, Sun. 12 PM–5 PM. Admission: Free. The Amon Carter Museum was established to house his personal collection of paintings and sculpture by Frederic Remington and Charles M. Russell; the mission has since expanded to collect, preserve, and exhibit the finest examples of American art. The museum houses one of the nation's preeminent collections of American art, from works by the early 19th-century artist-explorers through those of the mid-20th-century modernists and up to the work of contemporary photographers. The Carter Museum has a rare and illustrated book collection, paintings, and nearly 4,000 square feet of photography gallery space. On-site is a library of more than 100,000 items; it is one of the nation's premier centers for the advanced study of American art, photography, and history. The museum offers guided tours, gallery talks, Family Fundays, and reading groups for all of its audiences. Hands-on interactive art carts are in the galleries on selected weekday and weekend afternoons.

Bass Hall. Monica Prochnow

Bass Performance Hall (817-212-4325; www.basshall.com) 525 Commerce Street, Fort Worth 76102. Bass Hall hosts a variety of theatrical, operatic, orchestral, and ballet performances by large-name, in-house, and traveling companies and artists. Even off-Broadway shows have been featured there. See website or call ahead for upcoming performances, dates, times, locations, and ticket pricing.

Casa Mañana. Monica Prochnow

Casa Mañana Theatre (817-332-2272; www.casamanana.org) 3101 West Lancaster Avenue, Fort Worth 76107. Casa Mañana is a historic amphitheater in Fort Worth that has a variety of musical theater performances, music concerts, and children's plays that provide family-friendly programming. See website or call ahead for upcoming performances, dates, times, and ticket pricing.

Fort Worth Botanic Garden (817-871-7686; www.fwbg.org) 3220 Botanic Garden Boulevard, Fort Worth 76107. Open: Daily, 8 AM–dusk. Admission: The main garden areas are free; the Japanese Garden charges $5; and Tropical Conservatory costs $1. For breathtaking natural beauty in all four seasons, visit the Fort Worth Botanic Garden. It features a Japanese garden, two rose gardens, a perennial garden, a fragrance garden, a Texas native garden, a tropical conservatory, and countless outdoor sculptures; all 109 acres of this space are inspiring. Bring your comfy shoes, as you will walk quite a bit, but also bring your camera to capture all that your eye can behold. The Japanese garden, which can bring even the weariest visitor peace and relaxation, is home to annual festivals in fall and

Fort Worth Botanic Garden. Monica Prochnow

Fort Worth Botanic Garden. Monica Prochnow

Fort Worth Botanic Garden. Monica Prochnow

spring that celebrate the spectacular colors with dance, music, martial arts demonstrations, papermaking, and tea ceremonies. Feed the koi in the ponds and then visit the 10,000-square-foot conservatory to see orchids, bromeliads, and exotic trees from around the world. The botanic gardens are also home to summertime music concerts. There are too many stunning scenes to mention here.

Fort Worth Museum of Science and History (817-255-9300; www.fwmuseum.org) 1600 Gendy St., Fort Worth 76107. Open: Daily, 10 AM–5 PM. Admission: Varies according to attraction; combo ticket prices available. Recently renovated and expanded, the Fort Worth Museum of Science and History is a favorite among Fort Worth locals, particularly those with families. The museum is home to more than 175,000 historical and scientific objects and has thousands of botany, entomology, malacology, ornithology, mineralogy, herpetology, mammalogy, invertebrate zoology, meteoritic, and paleontology specimens. It is also involved in local paleontological digs and is continuously adding fossils and other finds. Home to the William Green Memorial Library, which contains more than 6,000 volumes, its materials include information on Texas and Fort Worth–related specimens.

The museum provides plenty of hands-on activities for young visitors, with evolving and permanent exhibits focusing on the environment, Hopi Kachina dolls, bird eggs, Texas butterflies and moths, World War I aviation, astronomy, and more. Visitors can explore the museum, see a show in the planetarium, or watch a film in the Omni Theater.

Fort Worth Opera (817-731-0726; www.fwopera.org), 1300 Gendy Street, Fort Worth 76107. See website or call ahead for upcoming performances, dates, times, and ticket pricing.

Kimbell Art Museum. Monica Prochnow

Fort Worth Symphony Orchestra (817-665-6000; www.fwsymphony.org). See website or call ahead for upcoming performances, dates, times, locations, and ticket pricing.

Kimbell Art Museum (817-332-8451; www.kimbellart.org), 3333 Camp Bowie West Boulevard, Fort Worth 76107. Open Tues. through Thurs. and Sat. 10 AM–5 PM, Fri. 12 PM–8 PM, Sun. 12 PM–5 PM. Admission: The museum's permanent collection is free; there is a charge for special exhibitions; half-price exhibition admission is offered on Tuesdays all day and Fridays from 5 PM–8 PM. Although the Kimbell has only a small collection of about 350 pieces, its works are from around the globe and extend from antiquity to contemporary time. The Kimbell collection focuses on European, Asian, African, Pre-Columbian, and Oceanic art. It also brings in exhibits from around the world, featuring both historically significant and well-known artists and their work.

The Kimbell recently purchased Michelangelo's painting *The Torment of Saint Anthony* for its permanent collection.

Log Cabin Village (817-392-5881; www.logcabinvillage.org), 2100 Log Cabin Village Lane, Fort Worth 76109. Open Tues. through Fri. 9 AM–4 PM, Sat. and Sun. 1 PM–5 PM. Admission: Age 18+ $4.50, age 4–17 and 65+ $4, children 3 and under free. The Log Cabin Village is a living history museum that connects visitors to life in Texas during the 19th century. The village is comprised of various log cabin structures, including a one-room schoolhouse, a blacksmith shop, a mill, and several homes, complete with artifacts. Be mindful of the weather when attending, as the village is outdoors.

Modern Art Museum of Fort Worth (The Modern) (817-738-9215; www.mamfw.org) 3200 Darnell Street, Fort Worth 76107. Open: Tues. through Sat. 10 AM–5 PM, Sun. 11 AM–

Meteorite from the Monnig Meteorite Gallery at TCU in Fort Worth. © Monnig Meteorite Gallery, photograph by Geoffrey Notkin

5 PM, open later some days on a seasonal basis. Admission: General $10, students with ID and seniors (60+) $4, children 12 and under free; All admissions are free on the first Sunday of every month and half-price every Wednesday.

Monnig Meteorite Gallery at TCU (monnigmuseum.tcu.edu) 2950 W. Bowie, Fort Worth 76109. Open: Tues. through Fri. 1 PM–4 PM, Sat. 9 AM–4 PM. Admission: Free. The Monnig Meteorite Gallery, which contains over 1,450 different meteorites, is located on the Texas Christian University campus. Meteorites are rocks and rock fragments that orbit in space and fall to the earth; they fascinated museum founder Oscar E. Monnig, a wealthy Fort Worth businessman. A few years before his passing, Monnig donated his collection of meteorites to the university, and TCU has not only maintained it but also increased the size of the collection for both visitors and scientists to see and study. Visitors are invited to see the meteorites and walk through the museum at their own pace or borrow an audio wand for a narrated tour. The museum is located in the Sid Richardson Science Building at the corner of West Bowie Street and Cockrell.

National Cowboys of Color Museum (817-534-8801; www.cowboysofcolor.org) 3400 Mount Vernon Avenue, Fort Worth 76103. Open: Wed. through Sat. 11 AM–6 PM. Admission: Adults $6, seniors $4, students with ID $3, children 5 and under free.

Sid Richardson Museum. Monica Prochnow

National Cowgirl Museum and Hall of Fame (817-336-4475; www.cowgirl.net) 1720 Gendy Street, Fort Worth 76107. Open: Tues. through Sun. 10 AM–5 PM. Admission: Adults $10, seniors (60+) $8, children 3-12 $8, children 2 and under free with paid adult; Parking $5.

Sid Richardson Museum (817-332-6554; www.sidrmuseum.org) 309 Main Street, Fort Worth 76102. Open: Mon. through Thurs. 9 AM–5 PM, Fri. and Sat. 9 AM–8 PM, Sun. 12 PM–5 PM. Admission: Free. One of the finest and most focused collections of Western art in America, the Sid Richardson Museum features paintings of the American west by Frederic Remington, Charles M. Russell, and other artists such as Western landscapists (Albert Bierstadt, Thomas Moran), the pre–Civil war documentarians (George Catlin, Karl Bodmer, Alfred Jacob Miller, Paul Kane, Charles Wimar), and late 19th-century artists including Gilbert Gaul, Peter Moran, and Charles F. Browne. The museum also holds in its permanent collection a lot of paintings with action or suspense by Charles Schreyvogel, Oscar E. Berninghaus, Frank Tenney Johnson, William R. Leigh, and Edwin W. Deming. The Museum Store offers bronze reproductions of works, prints on canvas, prints, books, and postcards, as well as CDs, tapes, jewelry, puzzles, and handmade lariat baskets.

Texas Ballet Theater (817-763-0207; www.texasballettheater.org) 6845 Green Oaks Road, Fort Worth 76116. The Texas Ballet Theater is the preeminent professional dance company in North Texas. Employing 38 professional dancers and operating two ballet academies in both Dallas and Fort Worth, the Texas Ballet Theater is a cornerstone of the local arts community. This world-class company performs in the Winspear Opera House located in the

The Modern Art Museum of Fort Worth. Fort Worth CVB

National Cowgirl Museum and Hall of Fame. Fort Worth CVB

AT&T Performing Arts Center in Dallas and the Bass Performance Hall in Fort Worth and has long performance seasons, starting in the fall and lasting into early summer. While the performances change often, one constant remains—the Texas Ballet Theater performs Tchaikovsky's famous *The Nutcracker* to excited audiences each year. For a listing of performances, consult the website. Prices vary.

Texas Cowboy Hall of Fame (817-626-7131; www.texascowboyhalloffame.org) 128 East Exchange, Fort Worth 76164. Open: Mon. through Thurs. 10 AM–6 PM, Fri. and Sat. 10 AM–7 PM, Sun. 11 AM–5 PM. Admission: Adults $5, seniors (60+) $4, children 5-12 $3, children 4 and under free, military with active or retired ID free (family not included). Located in the Stockyards in historic Barn A, the Texas Cowboy Hall of Fame honors Texas men and women who have excelled in the sport and business of rodeo and/or proudly exhibited the western lifestyle. Past inductees include Nolan Ryan, Tommy Lee Jones, Trevor Brazile, Don Edwards, George Strait, Lane Frost, Ty Murray, Barry Corbin, Red Steagall, Tuff Hedeman, J. J. Hampton (17-time PWRA World Champion), Charmayne James, and Don Gay (8-time PRCA World Champion Bull Rider). Each inductee has a booth filled with personal memorabilia. There is a permanent Chisholm Trail Exhibit and a 1933 Cadillac Coupe from the millionaire philanthropist Amon G. Carter. The museum is also home of the Sterquell Wagon Collection, featuring more than 60 wagons, buggies, and sleighs that chronicle not only the evolution of transportation but also the cowboy lifestyle itself. The barn that houses the museum was originally built in 1888, and held 3,000 horses and mules at any one time. The bricks, columns, metal doors, catwalks, and cinder blocks in the interior are all original architectural elements.

PLANO

Angelika Film Center & Cafe (972-943-1300; angelikafilmcenter.com) 7205 Bishop Road, Plano 75024-3627. Located in the Shops at Legacy, the Plano location of the Angelika is dedicated to artistic and independent cinema in North Texas on five screens. The Angelika plays a diverse mix of independent films and has a sleek and chic vibe and is reminiscent of its New York City counterpart in SoHo. The theater is a great place to meet friends, take in a stunning performance, or enjoy light but gourmet fare at the café or in the lounge on the second floor, which has far more sophisticated offerings than the typical popcorn-and-cola menu at most theaters. Enjoy a toasted panini, a cheese plate, elegant hors d'oeuvres, or munch on a dessert bar with your cappuccino. Discuss filmography over a glass of wine, champagne, or beer, which can be packed into an ice bucket to take inside the auditorium. Tickets are under $10 each, and discounts are given for seniors and children. Consult the website for the current and future roster of movie listings. Visit Angelika's second location in Dallas.

Insider tip: Validated parking is available in all of the Sundance parking lots, including the Chisholm Trail parking lot (3rd, 4th, Main, and Houston streets are the borders), as well as in the Towers garage located on Commerce St. and 2nd.

5

Restaurants, Food Purveyors, and Nightlife

Enjoying Our Place at the Top of the Food Chain

According to the Texas Restaurant Association, there are so many restaurants in the Dallas–Fort Worth area, a person could eat at a new place every day for breakfast, lunch, and dinner for more than seven years and never be at the same eatery twice. That translates into approximately 7,000-plus restaurants in DFW, with new ones opening up every day. That also means there are more restaurants per capita than in any other city in America, and, as a result, the locals who have all of these culinary options at their disposal love dining out. Estimates by the association reveal that the average DFW resident dines out approximately 4.3 times per week.

Jim White, local food critic, radio personality, and one of the founders of Savor Dallas, a very chic annual food and wine event that takes place every March, happily shared his knowledge of food in Texas. The year 1980, he noted, marked a sea change in the local cuisine scene. Before then, the Metroplex was filled with cafeterias, old-fashioned steakhouses, and snooty fine-dining restaurants that were expensive and pretentious.

Southwestern cuisine came into fashion, and the aura of the local restaurants changed. This new cuisine brought about an unprecedented focus on regional tastes, and menus everywhere were reinvented. It gave DFW the momentum to attract new chefs and new cuisines, and they, for the first time, were given a license to experiment with regional flavors and ingredients.

It is not surprising, then, that the DFW area has an enormous selection of barbeque, Tex-Mex, and Mexican food restaurants, which is reflective of the area's historical and cultural heritage. However there are many ethnically diverse restaurants opening up and thriving in DFW; they reflect the cultural diversity of the area and the locals are willing to support them.

Rolling well into the new century, restaurants and purveyors have continued to evolve. There is a recent trend in focusing on fresh, seasonal, and local ingredients, which means that the once-staid menus of yesteryear, even for the older restaurants, are long gone. Restaurant menus are now unpredictable and changing to reflect an emphasis on seasonal or organic produce, free-range meats, refined regional flavors, and a strong support of local farmers and cattle ranchers. The restaurants recommended in this guide, for the

vinaigrette and the blueberry gallette, pear tart or lemon bars for dessert. The atmosphere is communal, with doily-like knitted tablecloths and curtains, mismatched dinette sets, dinnerware, napkins, and glasses. The restaurant, which just opened in 2009, has quite a following in Arlington already.

Prince Lebanese Grill (817-469-1811; www.princelebanesegrill.com) 502 West Randol Mill Road, Arlington 76011. Open: Mon. through Sat. 11 AM—9 PM, closed Sun. This Middle Eastern restaurant situated in a converted Sonic drive-in may not look like much on the outside, but inside is where some darn good food awaits. Prince Lebanese Grill has creamy hummus with a side order of zing and equally smooth baba ghanoush that is unforgettable. Start the meal with a Mazza Plate; it's a sampler appetizer that is big enough for a meal; it includes hummus and baba ghanoush, plus a healthy helping of startling fresh and crisp tabouli, dolmas, and warm pita bread for scooping. Move on to the Shawarma Plate with a choice of chicken or beef and topped with grilled tomatoes and onions, lemon, garlic, and a kick to boot. The falafel appetizer, which is also served fresh, is also a good side dish to add to any meal. The Prince Lebanese Special, a five-meat-and-kabob sampler plate, is great for the carnivore or the indecisive. Finish the meal with a serving of sweet and delicately crafted baklava, or the get the Dessert Sampler, which features three sweet delicacies. Wash dessert down with a cup of Turkish coffee, but know that this small, espresso-sized serving packs a powerful punch. The restaurant offers a small patio for outside dining, online coupons, and even an Internet ordering system for to-go orders—perfect for anyone headed to either the Cowboys or Rangers stadiums about 1 mile away who want to forgo the "sports food" served there.

Dallas

Cosmic Café (214-521-6157; www.cosmic cafedallas.com) 2912 Oak Lawn, Dallas 75219. Open: Mon. through Thurs. 11 AM—10:30 PM, Fri. and Sat. 11 AM—11 PM, Sun. 12 PM—10 PM. Rated "Best Vegetarian Restaurant" for nine years by the *Dallas Observer*, Cosmic Café is a haven for vegetarians amid an urban jungle of steaks, but even meat-eaters will love their menu. Try the Herban Renewal—avocado, cream cheese, spinach, mushrooms, mozzarella, and herbs on naan, or veggie-only versions of favorites such as quesadillas, enchiladas, burgers, and pizza. They also offer many Indian favorites like curried vegetables, dahl, samosas, and basmati rice. There are several beverage options for you to wash down your veggies—natural sodas, ginger beer, fresh juices, smoothies, shakes, beer, and wine.

Five Sixty by Wolfgang Puck (214-741-5560; www.wolfgangpuck.com/restaurants /fine-dining/3917) 300 Reunion Boulevard, Dallas 75202. Dinner: Mon. through Thurs. 5:30 PM—10 PM, Fri. and Sat. 5:30 PM—11 PM, closed Sun. Happy Hour: Mon. through Fri. 5 PM—7 PM. Five Sixty is that big ball in the sky, and no, not the sun. It's the restaurant that is located in the large ball of lights atop Reunion Tower, 560 feet up into

Five Sixty Dallas Courtesy of Five Sixty

Five Sixty Dallas Courtesy of Five Sixty

the air. Celebrity chef Wolfgang Puck's Five Sixty, his premiere fine dining restaurant, offers stunning panoramic view of Dallas, and an equally sophisticated Asian-inspired cuisine to match. Ride the elevator as it opens up into the center of the restaurant and step out to soak up the atmosphere, graciously provided by floor-to-ceiling glass walls. If you're not too busy gawking at the gorgeous skyline, notice the restaurant slowly revolves for a constantly changing view of the city below. Eat in the main dining area or have a cocktail in either of the two bars that also look out into the city; wine aficionados can select a bottle of wine from any of the 400-plus labels offered or enjoy the dozen or so sake options and have a relaxing sip before dinner. The Steamed Wild King Salmon and the Grilled Mongolian Lamb Chops are both excellent. Looking for something a little different? The Green Thai Seafood Curry with Prawns, Halibut, Scallops, and Coconut Chutney require two staffers just to present and serve the dish (dinner and a show!), perfect for impressing that certain someone. If you are already snuggly, try the 32 oz. Double Cut Bone-In Prime Beef Rib Chop For Two, served with Yu Choi, Garlic Chives, Wasabi-Armagnac Peppercorn Sauce, and Drunken Noodles; it is perfect date-night dinner, just right for sharing. Finish the evening with a Baked Alaska or Yuzu Cheesecake Brûlée, dripped with a cherry reduction glaze and fresh cherries. Know that this place has a dress code—business casual. That translates into a collared shirt for gentlemen; jeans are acceptable as long as they are not torn. Sandals or flip-flops are not permissible. Reservations are recommended, and valet parking is available.

Hacienda on Henderson (214-515-9990; www.haciendaonhenderson.com) 2326 North Henderson Avenue, Dallas 75206. Open: Daily, 11 AM–2 AM. There are three words to describe this place: *tequila* and *high energy*. The Hacienda on Henderson specializes in both, with 40 tequilas available and several of them on tap kept at a crisp and cool 5 degrees—optimum for blending and sipping. This converted 1940s home-turned-restaurant/bar is all about drinking, eating, and having fun while doing it. Several mescal options are also offered in its adventurous drink menu. Look for the long list of specialty drinks, like the Spanish Fly cocktail, that can be ordered there, but where this place really shines is in its house margaritas, which are only $2 each during happy hour. Make sure to get some Tex-Mex with your drinks, either in the cozy dining room where you can watch the game on one of the televisions or in the large, festive patio outside. Our preference? Sit in the patio next to the water fountain and underneath the hanging plants for the best atmosphere and a bit of people-watching. Make sure to get there early for the best seats. Order the queso blanco to munch on and choose between the fajitas, which are tender and full of flavor, the surf-n-turf tacos, the spare ribs, or the brisket tacos. The best thing about the Hacienda, however, is its late-night hours; it's open until 2 AM every day. Hacienda also has a special Sunday brunch menu with generous mimosas that keep flowing all day. There is live music on weekends, and parking is exclusively valet. The website offers online to-go ordering, but we cannot figure out why anyone would want to skip out on this fun place.

La Duni Latin Café (214-520-7300; www .laduni.com) 4620 McKinney Avenue, Dallas 75205. La Duni offers something for everyone—from fresh squeezed juices, a full breakfast menu, and an extensive list of espresso drinks to positively sinful desserts like Pastel de Banano y Trufa Chocolate de Maracaibo and blended tropical fruit smoothies. Savor the authentic foods and drinks and participate in the traditions and customs that have been passed from generation to generation of passionate Latin families. Hours vary by location and meal—check website or call ahead; La Duni does not accept reservations.

Rathbun's Blue Plate Kitchen (214-890-1103; www.kentrathbun.com/blueplate/dallas) Preston Center, 6130 Luther Lane, Dallas 75225. Chef Kent Rathbun may tout his Blue Plate Kitchen as comfort cuisine, but this home cooking is upscale; it's akin to eating at Grandma's house but using the good china and being dressed up in Sunday duds. Start the meal with either the Polenta Crusted Fried Green Tomatoes or the Wood Roasted Cheesy Bread, cooked in rosemary olive oil and ricotta, as an appetizer. The Texas Pecan Crusted Trout served with roasted spaghetti squash and Jim Beam butter sauce may sound simple, but the bourbon sauce and the squash puree are an incredible combination, giving the entrée a sweet, then crunchy, and then smooth texture within each bite. Not a seafood fan? No problem. The full rack of Jasper Ribs, served with baked potato salad, provides the right combination of smoky and salty for a hearty flavor. Regardless of which entrée you order, make sure to get a side of the Brazos Valley Cheddar Mac 'n' Cheese to go with it; it's full of creamy goodness baked with crunchy cheese crumbles on the top for a perfect texture and crust that isn't too heavy. End the meal with a S'mores Pie or an Apple Tart. If all of this talk of home cooking makes you remember Aunt Bessie's overpowering perfume a little too well, order a John Daly (iced tea, lemonade, citron, and vodka), cognac, port, or anything off the long wine menu, and it can make even the stoic homesick. While Rathbun's does offer a separate kids' menu, it really isn't the place for children. Menus differ among lunch, dinner, and Sunday brunch, and they are all wonderful, even if south-ern-style cooking doesn't match your own memory of home. Know that this upscale restaurant also comes with an upscale price.

Rusty Taco (214-613-0508; www.therusty taco.com) 4802 Greenville Avenue, Dallas 75206. Open: Mon. through Fri. 7 AM to 10 PM, Sat. 8 AM to 10 PM, Sun. 8 AM to 8 PM. Rusty Taco is the new, hip place to be seen on Greenville Avenue in Dallas, and $2 tacos are the reason. This taqueria has a limited menu of just nine regular tacos, but the meat and veggie choices within them are quite wide—ground beef, roasted pork, beef or chicken fajita-style meat, brisket, fish, and shrimp. Order anywhere between three and five for a meal, as they are somewhat small, but perfect for sampling the different flavors that the Rusty Taco offers. Order a side of chips and salsa for $1 or upgrade to guacamole or queso dip for $3. They also have breakfast tacos in potato, chorizo, jalapeño sausage, or bacon, made with egg and cheese for the early riser and served with either fresh corn or flour tortillas. Margaritas pair with their tacos beautifully, and they are the most expensive item on the menu at only $5 each, or have a beer from their list of domestic and foreign brews. The staff recommends the #5 (brisket), the #7 (fish), and the #9 (anchiote pork), but our faves are definitely the #5 and the #2 (roasted pork). The Rusty Taco is located inside a converted Just Brakes building. The decor maintains its unapologetically cool "garage chic," and even the soda fountain and utensil holders rest on top of Craftsman tool chests. On nice days, the staff opens up the sliding garage doors for cool breezes.

Samar by Stephan Pyles (214-922-9922; www.samarrestaurant.com) 2100 Ross Avenue, Dallas 75201. Lunch: Mon. through Fri. 11 AM to 2 PM. Dinner: Mon. through Wed. 5 PM–10:30 PM, Thurs. through Sat. 5 PM–11 PM. Bar: Mon. through Wed. 4

PM–12 AM, Thurs. through Sat. 4 PM–1 AM. Valet parking available beginning at 6 PM. The culinary cognoscenti of Dallas cannot say enough good things about this place or about Chef Stephan Pyles, who has a long-standing reputation for being on the cutting edge in the local restaurant scene, and it is easy to taste why. The food, served in small tapas-style portions, allows diners to savor incredible international flavors from India, Spain, and Eastern Mediterranean countries all at once. The menus are organized by geography and evolve with the seasons, allowing the staff to serve the freshest of produce and meat at their peak times. Each of the three sections feature salads, seafood, meat, and vegetarian options. The Patatas y Chorizo con Huevo Orgánico (potatoes and chorizo with fried Motley Farm organic egg and Hudson Valley foie gras), the Ajo Blanco Malagueño (almond gazpacho with liquid grapes), and the Croquetas del Cangrejo (Peekytoe crab fritters)—a favorite of many locals—hail from Spain. Traveling across the menu to India is a selection of chutney and freshly baked naan from their Bread Bar served from an authentic gas-fired tandoor oven in an open kitchen. The Tandoori Gobi ka Phool (saffron and cumin infused tri-colored cauliflower), the Mumbai ka Badi Jhinga (tiger prawns), and the Murgh Makhani (tandoori chicken butter masala with tomatoes and fenugreek) will be sure to please. On the final leg of the Samar journey, culinary travelers can be whisked away to the Mediterranean with the Salata Hundba maà Shumar (endive-orange salad with fennel, pecan labne and sumac) and the Halloum Meshwe Zahrat Laàteen (fried haloumi with green olive–pomegranate salad). The restaurant has both private and communal dining, a tented terrace, and a hookah lounge with plenty of cushions, couches, and candlelight that encircle a fire pit and water feature. Between the views of downtown and the arts district and its

high-energy atmosphere, dining at Samar is not just a meal but an experience. Samar was named best new restaurant in 2009 by the *Dallas Morning News* and given positive reviews in the *Wall Street Journal*. Metered and lot parking available at lunch. Validated parking (up to two hours) is available for guests who park in the garage.

Sonny Bryan's Smokehouse Barbeque (214-744-1610; www.sonnybryans.com) 302 North Market Street, Dallas 75202. Texans do not mince words when it comes to barbeque, which is why it is so remarkable that since 1958 Sonny Bryan's Smokehouse has been serving Dallas, Richardson, Irving, and Fort Worth locals at their various locations, and it has still maintained its status as a local favorite. Featured in *People* and *Zagat's*, as well as the Travel Channel and the Food Network, this unassuming restaurant with delicious food at reasonable prices has been serving up its simple menu of barbequed meats to a packed house every day. It's tough to choose between the pulled pork, sausage, ham, turkey, chicken, pulled chicken, ribs, or beef brisket, and the meats can be served in sandwiches, on platters, or on huge baked potatoes. A warmed sweet sauce comes on the side, and all sandwiches and certain dinner platters come with two sides, such as barbequed beans (smoky and delicious), coleslaw, French fries, macaroni and cheese (addictive), and fresh potato salad (crisp and zingy). Some of the locations' menus vary slightly, with others offering fried catfish, chicken-fried steak, po'boy sandwiches, salads, and Frito pie, in addition to the barbeque. Wash it down with sweet tea, which can be purchased in gallon-size containers. Meats can be ordered online through their website and can also be ordered by the pound or for catering options.

The Magic Time Machine (972-980-1903; www.magictimemachine.com) 5003

Beltline Drive, Addison 75254. Like its San Antonio counterpart, the Addison location of the Magic Time Machine is all about the novelty. Whether you visit the restaurant portion downstairs or the bars upstairs, the place looks like a yard sale that has spiraled out of control. The furniture is mismatched and comfortable but definitely a mix of the corduroy, plaid, stripe, and retro trends of decades past. The waitstaff is also a bit kooky, and you can be served by Captain Jack Sparrow, Woody the Sheriff, Wonder Woman, and Indiana Jones, dishing up delicious entrées like the Slow Roasted Prime Rib, Hand Cut Fresh Salmon, and an array of fresh seafood dishes. We even dare you to order the house specialty, the Roman Orgy, a pile of fresh fruits, veggies, and the rest of the kitchen sink, brought out with a song. Yes, Spiderman, Dr. Evil, Little Red Riding Hood, and even Dora the Explorer will sing to you as they deliver your Roman Orgy. Go there for a cocktail without the kids, and order a Magic Potion, which comes in red, blue, green, yellow, and ugly; it arrives lit up and bubbling with dry ice. If you don't leave this place smiling, check your pulse.

The Mansion Restaurant (214-443-4747; www.mansiononturtlecreek.com/dine1.cfm) 2821 Turtle Creek Boulevard, Dallas 75219. Nestled within the Mansion on Turtle Creek, you will find the area's only five-star dining establishment. With a menu that is inviting and approachable, expensive yet attainable, the Mansion Restaurant turns only the freshest and finest ingredients into savory dishes, highlighting their best flavors. Its sleek design and beautiful art contribute to the warm ambience, and you should definitely enjoy some time dining or lounging on the veranda or near the Palladian windows with views of the terrace. The asparagus and wild mushroom risotto is absolutely heavenly. Call for reservations; not recommended for children.

Just a sampling of the snarky signage inside Twisted Root Burger Co. Courtesy of Twisted Root Burger Co.

Denton County Independent Hamburger Co. Monica Prochnow

Twisted Root Burger Co. (214-741-7668; www.twistedrootburgerco.com) 2615 Commerce Street, Dallas 75226. This fun and funky hamburger joint is owned and operated by three former gourmet restaurant chefs, and the burgers at Twisted Root Burger reflect that level of excellence. Diners can order hefty half-pound burgers in traditional beef, venison, ostrich, buffalo, turkey, or spicy veggie. Burgers can be made to order or crafted into one of their specialty items like the Chipotle, Guac & Cheddar Burger w/ Fried Onions, the Peppercorn Ranch & Bacon Burger, or the Green Chile, Guacamole & Pepperjack Burger. Twisted Root also serves hot dogs made from 100 percent Angus beef that are as hearty and filling as their burger counterparts. Order a side of sweet potato chips, onion ring strings, twisted fries, fried green beans, or fried pickles to accompany your burger or dog. Salads and bun-free burgers are also served here, as are root beer floats and creamy milkshakes in vanilla, chocolate, peanut butter, cookie dough, or Oreo. For the 21-and-up crowd,

"adult milkshakes" are available in Banana-Bailey's or Amaretto-Oreo, as well as a healthy selection of shivering cold beer. The restaurant also makes its own root beers, traditional and amaretto-style, as well as its own ketchup, and the freshness and vibrancy of the flavors, even in the soda, is remarkable. The music playing in the backdrop is energetic, and the environment is spirited—a great scene for a great burger. There are several locations: two in Dallas, one in Richardson, and one in Roanoke; call for hours at each location.

Denton

Denton County Independent Hamburger Co. (940-383-1022) 113 West Hickory Street, Denton 76201. Open: Mon. through Sat. 11 AM–8 PM. Denton County Independent Hamburger Co. has been an institution in Denton since 1977. Wear short sleeves because their generous, thick burgers are so juicy they will drip into your hand and down your arm. It's a tough call as to which is the best burger in the joint—the barbeque or the chili burger; they are made from the fresh beef ground in-house daily. The cheeseburgers come with a mound of grated cheddar cheese. They can also make custom-built burgers, and there is an array of toppings, both usual and atypical, that you can request, including a variety of shakers of salts and seasonings. Every meal comes with all-you-can-eat fries and beans that have been slow-cooked all day. The fries are old-fashioned (read: unpeeled and wedged, crisp but not hard), salted perfectly and cut from fresh potatoes each day. Denton Hamburger Co. is always busy and you may even have to wait five or 10 minutes, but the service is always fast, friendly and helpful, too. Mr. Kim Kitchens (no, we're not kidding), the owner, adores antiques and has decorated the walls with signs, old Denton-area photos, and other novelties, like Mr. T's 15-piece Deluxe

El Guapo's. Monica Prochnow

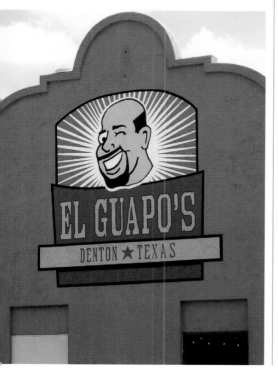

Jewelry Set and a steer skull. The eclectic charm also extends to the exterior of the building, as the facade of the restaurant is decorated with wood left over from an old barn that once stood on his family property. There is a second location at 715 Sunset Street, which serves beer and also has a drive-through window. Warning: Denton Hamburger Co. is cash only!

El Guapo's (940-566-5575; www.elguapos .com) 419 South Elm Street, Denton 76201. Open: Mon. through Fri. 11 AM–10 PM, Sat. and Sun. 11 AM–11 PM. El Guapo's is not a fancy Tex-Mex restaurant with overly posh decor or owned by a celebrity chef; instead, El Guapo's is a solid restaurant that serves hearty food and standard fare quickly and reasonably and with confidence—perfect for people who hate snooty restaurants and just want to get down to the business of eating a darn good meal. El Guapo's is a huge restaurant with an eight-page menu that contains a lunch section, a dinner section, a party platter section, a dessert section, a kids' menu, and even a "Choose Your Own Lunch" adventure with à la carte ordering at combo platter pricing. This place has it all, from the traditional burritos, tacos, enchiladas, fajitas, and rellenos to a few new twists like Santana's Supernatural Quesadillas made with fajita-style chicken, bacon, and chipotle or the Jefe's Jalapeño Stuffed Shrimp. What is it stuffed with, you may ask? Bacon, of course. Try the empanada appetizer for a surprisingly large filled pie with deliciously seasoned ground beef. Pair it with the Guapamole, which is served in three generously sized scoops for only $2.99, for serious chip-dipping. Also, make sure to ask for the homemade tortillas, still warm and soft. The Big Bad Burrito will leave you full and begging your belly for mercy, and the Ilada Parilla Asada, a chili-rubbed fajita steak topped with slices of fresh avocado, and accompanied by two cheese enchiladas, rice, and beans has so much food you'll feel like you're ripping them off. The El Guapote Feature for two is an excellent fajita dinner bargain meant to be shared by two people at only $24.99. It starts with a bowl of queso and chips, a double order of meat (beef, chicken, or combo), refried beans, Spanish rice, and fried ice cream for dessert. Full bar; plenty of parking.

Jupiter House Coffeehouse on the Square (940-387-7100; www.jupiterhousecoffee .net) 106 North Locust Street, Denton 76203. Open: Daily 6 AM–1 AM. Jupiter House Coffeehouse on the Square is the place for hipsters of all ages (and far more relaxed than, say, some not-to-be-mentioned national coffeehouse chains). Located on the town square that surrounds the city's courthouse, this planet-themed coffeehouse offers espresso and coffee drinks, smoothies (Pasteur's lawnmower, the Oppenheimer, and the staff recommended Tesla tofu-berry, which bears no resemblance to tofu at all), teas, milkshakes, organic juices, signature drinks (Caramel Comet and Jupiter's Nectar are both tasty), and fresh pastries that are out of this world. There are a few tables on the patio for people-watching and enjoying the sunshine. This is a great place to hang out, have a meeting, get some work done with the free Wi-Fi, or even read the local paper with a cup o' joe with minimal distractions. Along the walls are art pieces from various local artists, and the music inside is modern without being annoying. Even the bathrooms are cleverly decorated, as they are wallpapered with news articles about the planet Jupiter. The best part of this place, though, is the fact that it's open late, until 1 AM daily. Two locations, both in Denton.

Movie Tavern (Movie Line: 940-566-3456, Box Office: 940-483-1483; www.movie tavern.com/theaterlocations7/denton 4006.php) 916 West University Drive, Denton 76201. Tired of the boring "dinner and a movie" routine? The Movie Tavern kicks the same-ol' date night or family outing up to a new level. Buy a movie ticket, grab a menu, and stop by the full bar to sip on a cocktail. Arrive early and take the time to nuzzle a 38 oz. Tavern Tanker, filled with your choice of beer, or the Blue Thing, the house's signature margarita, or take it with you into the theater. The seating is comfortable—not cramped like a regular movie house. Each auditorium has either tiered or stadium seating, including executive high-back leather rocker chairs that scoot up to counter-style tables. This means the extra seats have been removed to allow for dining tables, and every seat has a perfect view of the screen with plenty of room to stretch. While the previews play, decide on an entrée, and a member of the waitstaff will take your order and deliver food directly to you in your seat. Of course, there's the traditional movie popcorn, sodas, and candy to be had, but the menu is surprisingly sophisticated. Order the tempura battered crab dumplings, chicken wing basket, fried pickles, or the fruit and cheese platter as an appetizer before deciding on a long list of entrées. Choose from 10-inch hand-tossed, thin-crust pizzas (the Godfather is always a winner), black-angus burgers, paninis, wraps, pitas (Cranberry, Pecan, and Chicken Pita is delightful), and delectable desserts like the warm, cinnamon-sprinkled apple crisp served with vanilla ice cream, caramel, and whipped cream. The Movie Tavern will always offer a great dinner and a fun outing—the hardest part will be deciding which movie to see. There are six locations throughout the Metroplex, with three in Fort Worth and one each in Denton, Bedford, and Arlington.

Rudy's Bar-B-Q (940-484-7839; www .rudys.com) 520 Interstate 35 Frontage Road, Denton 76205. Open: Sun. through Thurs. 6 AM–10 PM, Fri. and Sat. 6 AM–10:30 PM. Rudy's smokers are 100

It's all about the "sause" at Rudy's BBQ in Denton.
Laura Heymann

percent wood-fired with oak, a slower burning wood than the mesquite used by most other barbeque joints. Order your choice of brisket (lean or moist), turkey breast, pork loin, chopped beef, pork spare ribs, baby back ribs, chicken, sausage or jalapeño sausage, add some of Rudy's famous "Sause" (or "Sissy Sause"), and dinner is served. Note: There are no plates, but you get everything you need for your group on a big tray. Pass out the slips of wax paper and fix it up the way you like it, into a sandwich, with pickles and onions, or alone. If the weather's nice, enjoy a spot on the covered patio—kids love the oversize wooden chair outside as well (several can fit in at once). Other Metroplex locations include Arlington and Frisco.

Fort Worth

Babe's Chicken (817-447-3400; www .babeschicken.com) 120 South Main Street, Burleson 76028. Open: Mon. through Fri. 11 AM–2 PM and 5 PM–9 PM, Sat. and Sun. 11 AM–9 PM. Babe's is one of the best places to get home cookin,' possibly in the world. You order from six entrées: Fried chicken, chicken-fried steak, fried chicken tenders, smoked chicken, fried catfish, or pot roast.

Then your table fills up with all-you-can-eat sides of mashed potatoes, cream gravy, green beans, green salad, buttery kernel corn, and homemade biscuits for everyone. For dessert, they offer chocolate, lemon, or coconut meringue pies; southern-favorite banana pudding; or pineapple upside-down cake. The smoked chicken entrée and banana pudding dessert are highly recommended. Babe's has additional locations in Frisco, Carrollton, Garland, Roanoke (the original), Cedar Hill, Sanger, Arlington, and Granbury.

Chas. Kincaid Gro. Market (817-732-2881; www.kincaidshamburgers.com) 4901 Camp Bowie Boulevard, Fort Worth 76107. Open: Mon. through Sat. 11 AM–8 PM, Closed Sun. Burgers, burgers, and more burgers. Charles Kincaid Grocery and Market, now popularly known as Kincaid's Hamburgers, was established in 1946 as a neighborhood grocer with a full-service meat market. The butcher began cooking hamburgers to use up the excess beef, which he ground fresh daily, and business quickly evolved from a grocery store to a hamburger grill. Kincaid's hamburgers haven't changed at all over the years, as the hamburgers are still made from the best USDA choice boneless chuck available as well as the freshest of accompaniments. The beef is vegetarian-fed, and hormone-, antibiotic-, and preservative-free. Each hamburger is made with a half-pound beef patty, mustard, and freshly sliced lettuce, vine-ripened tomatoes, pickles, and yellow onions. They are served on locally baked Mrs. Baird's buns and with sliced, local Best Maid pickles. For those not into burgers, hot dogs, chili dogs, grilled cheese sandwiches, and BLT sandwiches are also on the menu. Fries, onion rings, deviled eggs, and an assortment of sides go well with any burger, as do the thick milkshakes. There are three locations in Fort Worth, one in Southlake, one in Arlington, and one in Weatherford.

Chef Point Café (817-656-0080; www.chef
pointcafe.org) 5901 Watauga Road, Watauga
76148. Open: Mon. through Thurs. 11 AM–
9 PM, Fri. 11 AM–10 PM, Sat. 7 AM–10 PM
(Breakfast Sat. 7am–11 AM), Sun. 10 AM–8
PM. Inside the ordinary-looking Conoco
Station on Watauga Road is Chef Franson's
dream, Chef Point Café, right next to the
aisles where sodas, cigarettes, and newspapers are sold. The large menu at the café
includes a wide range of entrées, from
basic dishes such as hamburgers and pizzas
to surprisingly sophisticated entrées like
the Stuffed New York Strip and Rack of
Lamb. Chef Franson's signature items are
What Nots—mushroom caps stuffed with
three cheeses and baked in a savory garlic
butter—and bread pudding served in a
warm cognac sauce, and of course, the
"Better than Sex" Fried Chicken, all of
which are get raves from locals. Cioppino
soup, a rare find in DFW, provides a flavorful blend of mussels, scallops, salmon,
clams, calamari, shrimp, and vegetables
cooked in a mix of tomato, broth, and white
wine, served in a toasted bread bowl. (The
soup was featured in *Cooking with Paula
Deen* magazine.) Our favorites are the
creamy lobster bisque, cooked to perfection, and anything on the Sunday brunch
menu. Chef Point Café was also featured on
NBC and the Food Network and in the *New
York Times* and *USA Today*.

Del Frisco's Double Eagle Steakhouse
(817-349-7194; www.delfriscos.com) 812
Main Street, Fort Worth 76102. Open: Mon.
through Thurs. 5 PM–10 PM, Fri. and Sat. 5
PM–11 PM, Sun. 5 PM–9 PM. Très chic! This
award-winning steakhouse has been given
more stars and awards than all the generals
in U.S. Army. There are two cornerstones to
the bliss that is dining at Del Friscos—
USDA Prime Beef and Australian Cold
Water Lobster Tail. The beef is prime-aged
and is only cut after it has been ordered.
Before dinner, try the zesty shrimp

remoulade before moving on to one of
many choices in select meats—filet mignon,
prime rib, strip steak, rib eyes, veal chops,
osso buco veal shank, prime porterhouse,
prime lamb, salmon, or lobster—all of
which are melt-in-your-mouth tender.
Also available are Alaskan king crab legs in
1- or 2-pound servings, stone crab claws
served with a Dijon mustard sauce, jumbo
shrimp, and even oysters on the half shell.
Order a side of sauteed mushrooms to driz-
zle atop of a steak, and perhaps a side of
asparagus as a veggie, both of which are
large enough to be shared around the table.
For dessert, try the crème brûlée for a mix
of creamy and custard-like sensation that
ends with a crunch; the Jack Daniel's bread
pudding, delicious but not overly sweet; or
the strawberries Romanoff, which contains
vanilla ice cream, fresh strawberries, and a
dazzling Grand Marnier sauce—all of which
are made fresh in-house daily. A staff som-
melier is available to assist with wine pair-
ings, or may we suggest the bloody Mary, a
local favorite? There's even a piano bar, a
dance floor, and a fireplace that glitters in
the dimly lit dining room. The service is
attentive but unobtrusive; valet parking is
available; dress is business casual. There
is a second location in downtown Dallas.

Dutch's Burgers (817-927-5522; www
.dutchshamburgers.com) 3009 South
University Drive, Fort Worth 76109. Open:
Mon. through Thurs. 11 AM–9 PM, Fri. and
Sat. 11 AM–10 PM, Sun. 11 AM–9 PM. Named
after the revered Texas Christian
University coach Dutch Meyers, who was
the head football coach from 1934 to 1952
and the head basketball coach from 1934
to 1937, it seems fitting that this cool college hangout is located directly across
from its alma mater. Serving hearty
burgers, thick shakes, and peppery
onion rings, Dutch's creates a winning
trifecta that is enough to land itself in a
hall of fame. The Linebacker is a huge

double-meat cheeseburger that comes with the standard fixings and a choice of fries, tater tots, and onion rings and will leave even the hungriest of appetites filled. The hickory barbeque and bacon burger is a first-stringer, but the bacon bleu cheese burger is the star that scores big. There is also a chicken and roasted green chile sandwich and a portobello veggie burger (roasted in balsamic vinegar) for those who prefer not to eat beef; you can also order the old Texas classic, Frito pie, for something different. The old building has lots of character, wooden floors and walls and counter seating along the window, as well as a lovely shaded patio in the back for outdoor dining and throwing back a few cold ones, even if it does face the parking lot. Speaking of parking, look for the small parking lot in back, because it is a tight fit everywhere else.

Eddie V's (817-336-8001; www.eddiev .com) 3100 West Seventh Street, Fort Worth 76107. Open: Daily at 4 PM. Eddie V's, located in a fashionable part of Fort Worth, is divided into two distinct areas—the bar and the restaurant—and each side is a great place to see and be seen. The restaurant side, complete with table linens and tuxe-doed servers, is shockingly unpretentious. Oh, but the food is serious. The menu is filled with a long list of sophisticated seafood appetizers and entrées typically found in island nations, brought in daily. Recommended are the filet of Atlantic salmon, which is served with an herb crust and a honey mustard vinaigrette, the Pacific ahi tuna steak, seared and covered in shi-itake mushrooms and ginger-soy sauce, and the Chilean sea bass, prepared in a lemon—white wine broth, sprinkled with garlic and scallions. The fish is buttery soft

Eddie V's. Monica Prochnow

and full of subtle notes. The filet mignon, New York strip, and rib eye are all tender and aged to perfection. The bar side fills up quickly, and the bartenders are fun and flirtatious. Whatever side you choose to visit, make sure to keep your wallet handy, as this place is expensive. But it definitely makes for a great night out, and your taste buds will thank you. Valet service is available for $5; live music nightly in the lounge.

Edelweiss German Restaurant (817-738-5934; www.edelweissrestaurant.com) 3801-A Southwest Boulevard, Fort Worth 76116. Open: Thurs. 4 PM–10 PM, Fri. and Sat. 4 PM–11 PM, Sun. 11 AM–8 PM, Closed Mon. through Wed. Willkommen! Texas has a strong German influence from one of its immigrant waves in the late 1800s–early 1900s, and Edelweiss is proud of keeping its cultural and culinary heritage alive in Fort Worth's cuisine scene. Owner, chef, and entertainer Chef Bernd has created a cozy dining experience and a traditional biergarten filled with paintings and Old World memorabilia. Straight from die Küche (the kitchen), the appetizers are delicious. The German fried onions and the potato pancakes are highly recommended. Follow it up with a bowl of soup—potato and cheese or Hungarian goulash—and then move on to an entrée. The sausage plate is best for getting a sample of bratwurst, knockwurst, or weisswurst, served with warm red cabbage, sauerkraut, and German fried potatoes. There are also schnitzels, as well as steaks, chicken, seafood, and even a light menu to choose from. Edelweiss has a full-service bar with a large selection of imported and domestic beverages, wines, spirits, and of course, German beers. Warsteiner, Spaten, Paulaner, Franziskaner, and Hacker-Pschorr are just a few of the several German brews offered, perfect for sipping while listening to the live entertainment. Listen to Chef Bernd, his wife, and other members of the family,

with the help of a few friends, play the accordion and sing German songs. Make sure to request "Edelweiss" played on the saw and then get on the dance floor to work off your meal. *Guten Appetit!*

Fuzzy's Taco Shop (817-831-8226; www.fuzzystacoshop.com) 2719 Race Street, Fort Worth 76111. Fuzzy's was opened in 2003 by four friends wanting good tacos, cheap eats, and lots of thirst-quenching beer, and this place has plenty of all three. Fuzzy's offers $2.25 draft beers and nothing on their menu is over $5.99. They have fresh tacos (chef's favorite), thick two-handed burritos, salads, sandwiches, enchiladas, fajitas, and even breakfast, but with slightly edgier flavors than traditional Mexican fare. Order the salted, spicy chips and the queso for an appetizer. The bowl of bubbling, melted white cheese is served in a bowl so big it requires the use of two hands to pick it up. Anything with chorizo is also a surefire hit, and so are the shrimp enchiladas. Most entrées are served with a side of delightfully sinful Latin fried potatoes. The menu features an array of grilled items for healthier dining options. There is also a kids' menu. Eat inside and watch the game or dine on the covered patio. This one-storefront operation has grown to a local chain of more than 15 locations (on the verge of going nationwide) in just a few short years; the additional locations are in Dallas, Denton, North Richland Hills, Arlington, Southlake, Richardson, Lewisville, Burleson, Plano, and Euless.

J&J Oyster Bar (817-335-2756; www.jjbluesbar.com/oysterbar.htm) 612 University Drive, Fort Worth 76107. Open: Sun. through Thurs. 11 AM–10 PM, Fri. and Sat. 11 AM–11 PM. The building that J&J Oyster Bar calls home is ugly, has minimal parking, tiny bathrooms, and is a converted old-school Taco Bell with cozy seating, but do not be fooled by this place's eyesore exterior. J&J's is a real seafood gem in the rough. The place specializes in oysters, and there's nothing tastier than a couple of dozen raw oysters served straight off the half shell and a cold Shiner Bock beer to wash it down. The fish tacos, served either grilled or fried, are excellent, and the gumbo or chowder are warm and satisfying on a cool winter day. The lemon pepper mahi-mahi, catfish, po'boys, and, when the season permits, boiled crawfish and Alaskan king crab legs are first-rate. Even frog legs are served here. Make sure to order a side of hush puppies for another dollar. J&J also offers lunch specials Monday through Friday.

Joe T. Garcia's (817-626-4356; www.joets .com) 2201 North Commerce Street, Fort Worth 76164. Open: Mon. through Thurs. 11 AM–2:30 PM and 5 PM–10 PM, Fri. and Sat. 11 AM–11 PM, Sun. 11 AM–10 PM. Joe T.'s could be the most adored restaurant in all of Fort Worth by locals—it will be recommended to you by everyone—frankly, we can't figure out why. On a Tex-Mex rating scale, the food is average, but the restaurant's atmosphere is an A+. The inside dining areas are pretty, but the outdoor garden seating with fountain and pool is absolutely gorgeous; try to sit outside if you can. Maybe it makes the food taste better?

Outdoor patio paradise at Joe T. Garcia's. Laura Heymann

Lucile's Stateside Bistro (817-738-4761; www.lucilesfortworth.com) 4700 Camp Bowie Boulevard, Fort Worth 76107. Open: Mon. through Thurs. 11:30 AM—10 PM, Fri. 11:30 AM—11 PM, Sat. 9 AM—11 PM, Sun. 9 AM—10 PM. Lucile's is an American classic eatery with a little bit of everything from pizza cooked in a wood-burning oven, salads, chicken-fried steak, sandwiches, steak, and homemade soups with an up-to-date flare. Where this place shines, however, is every August during Crabfest and every September/October during Lobsterama. Order the lobster bisque soup—it's rich and velvety with a hint of spice. They also have a daily specials board with unique entrées not found on the menu. The fried green tomato appetizer, tart and with a little zing, is a local favorite, as is the chicken-fried steak, thick and crispy and drowning in peppered gravy. On Friday and Saturday nights, Lucile's has a dessert station in the middle of the restaurant where orders of bananas Foster are assembled. The dark restaurant is lit up by the bright blue flame as the server brings the dessert to your table in a feat of spectacular showmanship. The bar features an array of award-winning martinis, a variety of wines, and bottled and draught beer. Service is efficient and friendly, but there may be a small wait to be seated.

Ol' South Pancake House (817-336-0311; www.olsouthpancakehouse.com) 1507 South University Drive, Fort Worth 76107. The Ol South Pancake House is a long-standing institution in Fort Worth located just north of Texas Christian University. This 24-hour old-school coffee shop has an extensive breakfast menu and also serves a selection of sandwiches, salads, burgers, and a variety of dinner entrées. You will have stars in your eyes over the German pancake, the signature dish. It is made from an egg-filled batter, cooked

and served as an oversized pancake. The server completes the entrée at the table, piling a cup of powdered sugar and dripping butter onto the hot pancake, then stirring in fresh-squeezed lemon juice together to create a sweet, warm sauce that rivals any lemon pie. This is a delicious dish for the adventurous or those with an extraordinary sweet tooth. Order a side of their extra-thick, hearty bacon to go with it. The pecan waffle, light and crisp, is made fresh in their on-site waffle iron and smothered in fresh pecans. Ol' South also has great pork chops and grilled catfish; look for the chicken-fried steak special Mondays through Fridays. The waitstaff is a mix of young, hip college students and waitresses that look they have been serving the locals for decades. Speaking of decades, the clientele is also a mix of young and old, and the older ones are folks who have clearly been eating there since its inception in 1962.

Riscky's Barbeque Deli and Catering (817-624-8662; www.risckys.com) 2314 Azle Avenue, Fort Worth 76164. Riscky's, regardless of whether you're talking about one of six of the barbeque houses or the

Riscky's Barbeque Deli and Catering Monica Prochnow

fine dining steakhouse, is a culinary institution in historic Fort Worth. The first location was opened in 1927 by Joe Riscky, who worked at the Armour Packing Company in the Stockyards. He obviously knew his way around a butcher shop, and Riscky served barbequed meats to the pickiest meat eaters around—the nearby ranchers and cattlemen, who also knew a thing or two about meat. He pleased the tough Cowtown crowd, a phenomenal feat unto itself, and Riscky knew he had a winner with his burgeoning restaurant. Whether you get the sliced beef, chopped beef, barbeque ham, ribs, sausage, smoked turkey, hot links, half chicken, or even the barbeque bologna (yes, really), it is all good. Meats are sold in "plates," which come with several sides like fresh potato salad, beans, and coleslaw, or are in sandwich form. The chopped beef sandwich, the ribs, and the sausage are local favorites. The meats are also available by the pound, and there is a little buckaroo menu, too. Wrapping up the meal with banana pudding complete with vanilla wafers is a Texas tradition. Riscky's Barbeque has three additional locations in Fort Worth: the Stockyards, Sundance Square, and on Camp Bowie Road, and another two in Benbrook and North Richland Hills. Riscky's Steakhouse is located on East Exchange Avenue just a few doors down from the famous Livestock Exchange Building. Know that the hours vary widely among the locations; call before visiting.

Sushi Zen Japanese Bistro (817-749-0900; www.gosushizen.com) 2600 East Southlake Boulevard, Southlake 76092. Open: Mon. through Thurs. 11 AM–2:30 PM and 5 PM–10 PM, Fri. 11 AM–2:30 PM and 5 PM–10:30 PM, Sat. 12 PM–10:30 PM, Sun. 12 PM–9:30 PM. If you ask local food critics about sushi in DFW, they may recommend one of the high-end locations in one of the downtown areas. This superb Southlake

bistro, however, is located in a small strip mall off State Highway 114. With more than 50 sushi, sashimi, and specialty roll items to choose from, they have an impressive, diverse menu with a lot of different seafood combinations and tastes. The seafood is tender and buttery soft and will melt in your mouth. Specialties include the volcano roll, the Keller fire roll (spicy), the S.H. 114 roll, the Vegas roll (yum), and our favorite, the white tiger roll. They also offer a small variety of seafood entrées, including a miso-glazed Chilean sea bass, barbeque ribs, bulgogi, and an unforgettable Japanese grilled seafood medley of shrimp, scallions, mussels, and squid. The atmosphere is serene and uncomplicated.

Uncle Julio's Fine Mexican Food (817-416-8416; www.unclejulios.com) 1301 William D. Tate Avenue, Grapevine 76051. Open: 11 AM–10:30 PM. Uncle Julio's is a casual hangout much adored by the locals, and with five locations across the Metroplex, in Dallas, Fort Worth, Grapevine, and Allen, it's easy to see why so many frequent it. Depending on the time you arrive, there may be a bit of a wait, so go to the bar and order the Swirl to pass the time. It's a generous blend of margarita and sangria served in a glass the size of a small fishbowl. Beyond its standard fare of tacos, enchiladas, and tamales, Uncle Julio's specializes in unusual flavors, offering marinated and mesquite grilled beef and chicken fajitas, ribs, quail, frog legs, and jumbo shrimp. There are three combo platters that are great for sampling a little of everything: tacos, tamales, chile rellenos, tamales, and enchiladas. The salsa is made from fire-roasted red peppers cooked slowly over the grill and then simmered in a pot all day long, which pairs nicely with the handmade tortillas, still warm and soft. But the hands-down, all-time favorites of the locals, time and time again are the steak fajitas, the costillas (ribs) slow roasted over mesquite, and the Guadalajara, the grilled jumbo shrimp brochette. The staff is fast and friendly, and if you catch it just right, you can get a whiff of the mouthwatering meats being grilled as you drive by on the highway.

Ye Olde Bull and Bush (817-731-9206; www.yeoldbullandbush.com) 2300 Montgomery Street, Fort Worth 76107. Open: Daily, 4 PM–2 AM. This place may disguise itself as a British pub, but it is really a drinking institution near downtown Fort Worth. They have a long list of international brews, ciders, and beers on tap including Guinness, Belhaven varieties, Boddingtons, Fullers varieties, Harp, Stella Artois, Paulaner, Smithwick, and more, as well as bottled beverages like Wyder's, Red Stripe, Carlsberg, Duchy Originals, Hoegaarden, and even novelty drinks like Monty Python's Holy Grail Ale. They also have a special-blends beer menu, featuring items like the black and tan, the shandy, the half and half, and other authentic British specialties. Come in to play darts, play some board games, or listen to the jukebox. There is also live music (sometimes a full band, other times bagpipe players) that you and even your dog, who is also invited to relax there, can enjoy. Sit on the porch and watch passersby and enjoy martini specials on Mondays or $2 well drinks all day on Tuesdays.

Yucatan Taco Stand Tequila Bar and Grill (817-924-8646; www.yucatantacostand1 .com) 909 West Magnolia, Fort Worth 76104. Open: Mon. through Wed. 11 AM–10 PM, Thurs. through Sat 11 AM–12 AM, Sun. 11 AM–10 PM. This is no ordinary Mexican food restaurant. The flavors experienced here are a mixture of bold and subtle tastes stemming from the unique mix of European, Caribbean, and Mayan influences of the Yucatan. Although surprisingly upscale for something that calls itself a taco stand, this place has a chic atmosphere with modern decor and a bar that will knock any tequila drinker's socks off. There are about 100 tequilas on the ever-evolving drink menu, as well as a range of rums, mescals, international wines, margaritas, and specialty house drinks. The drinks are a bit potent here, so brace yourself. If you can't settle on one tequila, try one of their flights—their name for their drink sampler tray—served with a sorbet course between tastes for palate cleansings. For an appetizer, try either the sweet fried plantains or the yucca fries, both of which are served with a roasted garlic aioli dipping sauce. The original tempura fish tacos are very lightly battered with a bit of crunch, the beef chorizo taco is assertive, and the tequila lime chicken taco has a lovely kick to it. The garlic shredded beef nachos will make your friends jealous, as will the handmade banana-leaf-wrapped tenderloin tamales. Yucatan Taco Stand also has patio dining and live guitar performances. Voted best of 2008 by *Fort Worth Weekly*.

Plano

Cafe Istanbul (972-398-2020; www.cafe -istanbul.net) 7300 Lone Star Drive, Suite 160C, Plano 75024. Open: Daily, 11 AM–11 PM. Cafe Istanbul is one of only a few Turkish restaurants in Dallas, but with a menu like this, not many others are needed. Every item on the menu is prepared using time-honored recipes, and the food is classic. Their lamb, which is the basis for many of their entrées, is marinated in olive oil, tender, and juicy. Their breadscome leavened and unleavened and arrive at the table steaming and poufy. Recommended are the Iskender, a lamb and beef pita; the pirzola, charbroiled lamb chops; and the steamed dumplings, filled with ground lamb, mint, and garlic yogurt sauce. The meze, the appetizer sampler plate, which is great for the indecisive, comes with several choices from dolmas, hummus, baba ganoush, eggplant salad, tabouleh, or acili (tomatoes, red bell peppers, olive oil, lemon, parsley, mint, and garlic). Wrap it up with baklava, rice pudding, or Turkish flan for dessert. Turkish tea or coffee is a must after dinner, or throw back a couple of shots of Raki for a nightcap. Join the café for belly dancing every Friday and Saturday night at 8:30 PM. Patio dining available in good weather. The Plano location is more upscale than its Dallas counterpart, but the food is amazing either way.

Jasper's (469-229-9111; www.jaspers -restaurant.com/plano) 7161 Bishop Rd, Ste G-1, Plano 75024. Jasper's, like its sister restaurant, Ken Rathbun's Blue Plate Kitchen of Dallas, is an upscale take on comfort food—this time it is backyard barbeque. Texas Peach Barbequed Pork Tenderloin is an interesting mix of hearty and delicate, the Hickory Grilled Black Angus Filet with Chunky Yukon Garlic Potatoes is a robust meal for the most serious of diners, and the pan-seared salmon served with a creamy mascarpone polenta and asparagus will leave you wanting more. Indulge in crispy calamari toasted in orange soy sauce, prosciutto-wrapped shrimp 'n' grits, or the Maytag blue cheese potato chips, which are crispy and topped off with blue cheese chunks and green onions. The Sunday brunch menu is just as flavorful with its Crabcake Benedict and White Truffle-Aged Gouda Omelette. For dessert, we recommend cherry limeade pie—tangy, sweet and refreshing after a smoky barbeque meal. There are also vegetarian options for those who do not eat meat or are just eating light. The restaurant has been featured in the *Wall Street Journal*, the *New York Times*, *Better Homes and Gardens*, *Esquire*, *Bon Appétit*, *Elle*, and *USA Today*, and on the *Today Show*. As you might imagine, it's a bit spendy to eat at Jasper's, but the lunch menu is almost identical and about half as expensive as the dinner menu.

Loft 610 (972-377-2500; www.loft610 .com/plano) 5760 Texas 121, Suite 175, Plano 75024. Open: Mon. through Tues. 11 AM–11 PM, Wed. 11 AM–12 AM, Thurs. 11 AM–1 AM, Fri. 11 AM–2 AM, Sat. 5 PM–2 AM, Sun. 10:30 AM–3 PM. Make a night of it at Loft 610—you can go for an elegant meal with great service and stay all night for cocktails and dancing. The restaurant is upscale and modern, and the wine list is extensive without the outrageous markup one would expect (the dinners are on the pricey side though, ranging from around $20–$40 per entrée). As an appetizer, try the bacon-wrapped jumbo shrimp with white Cheddar polenta and, for dinner, the pan-seared sea scallops with bacon-risotto and a pomegranate-citrus brown butter or the blue cheese–crusted prime rib eye steak with mixed fingerling potatoes and a balsamic–red wine sauce. The after-hours lounge features a live DJ who really gets the crowd moving. As with many restaurant/lounge combos, the clientele gets younger as the night progresses.

Ziziki's (972-943-8090; www.zizikis .com) 5809 Preston Road #578, Plano 75093. This place is one of the best places in the Metroplex to have gyros. They come stuffed with lamb and served with asparagus for tastes that would make Zeus himself proud. The sweet moussaka comes with tons of eggplant and seasoned lamb layered with béchamel and herbed potatoes, and the Ziziki bread (handmade pita with cheese, olive oil, garlic and Greek herbs) and the spanakopita are also amazing. Ziziki's also has about 30 Greek wines to complement any meal. Start with artichoke hummus or the trio appetizer platter for a little bit of everything, but end your meal with the baklava ice cream or the chocolate liqueur bundt cake. Ziziki's has separate lunch and dinner menus, and even a kids' and Sunday brunch menu. Try to dine outside on the patio next to their fountain if at all possible. There are two other locations, both in Dallas.

FOOD PURVEYORS

Arlington

BreadHaus (817-488-5223; www.bread haus.com) 700 West Dallas Road, Grapevine 76051. Open: Tues. through Fri. 9 AM–6 PM, Sat. 9 AM–4 PM. Drive through the neighborhood and follow that sweet bread smell, and you will find yourself in the parking lot of the BreadHaus. This family-owned bakery specializes in traditional rustic breads and sweets with a German flair and bakes from scratch using organic flours, grains, and seeds. Get there early in the morning for the best and still-warm selection. BreadHaus's treats—cookies, fruit bars, cakes, and more—do not contain added sugars, fats, or dairy, and the eggs come from cage-free chickens; they have a stunningly crisp and clear taste and not the sickeningly sweet flavor often found in store-bought treats. Take a couple of pretzels for the ride in the car; the crust is chewy and the inner dough is soft and sweet. The staff is eager to help and speaks both English and German.

Gnismer Farms (817-469-8704; www .gnismer.com) 3010 South Bowen Road,

Inside the BreadHaus in Grapevine. Monica Prochnow

Dalworthington Gardens 76016. If you haven't tasted farm-fresh vegetables you are in for a real treat. When you arrive at family-run Gnismer Farms, you will find tasty fruits and vegetables already harvested fresh from their garden for sale on their wagon, with selected crops available for "you-pick." Depending on the season, you may find cucumbers, peppers, blackberries, asparagus, garlic, onions, new potatoes, tomatoes, corn, eggplant, squash, lettuce, cantaloupe, and of course, Gnismer Farms' famous "you-pick" strawberries in the spring and the pumpkin patch in the fall.

Dallas

Central Market (214-234-7000; www .centralmarket.com) 5750 East Lovers Lane, Dallas 75206. Open: Daily, 8 AM–10 PM. Central Market is an Austin-based grocery store chain, but this is no run-of-the-mill store. Central Market prides itself items on high-quality, unique, and hard-to-find items from around the globe. This place contains wholesome goodness around every corner, and just walking through these always-busy stores can be overwhelming. Know that with organic products, an enormous selection of products, and made-to-order foods, this is not bargain shopping but an unforgettable experience. There are four locations within the Metroplex: Fort Worth, Plano, Dallas, and Southlake.

Chocolate Secrets (214-252-9801; www .chocolatesecrets.net) 3926 Oak Lawn Avenue, Dallas 75219. Open: Mon. through Thurs. 10 AM–9 PM, Fri. and Sat. 10 AM–11 PM, Sun. 11 AM–6 PM. At Chocolate Secrets life really is like a box of chocolates; you never know what goodies will await you whenever you walk through their door. Chocolate Secrets sells a large array of delectable chocolates that is awe-inspiring. Everything is handmade and hand-dipped, including the gourmet chocolates, truffles, bars, fondue, chocolate-dipped fruit, chocolate-coated nuts, and fudge, in dark chocolates, milk chocolates, and white chocolates from Saint Domingue, Venezuela, São Tomé, or Madagascar. The store also offers chocolates for cooking, drinking, and drizzling. To go with all of this chocolate madness, there are also boutique wines, beer, teas, crepes, and French pastries and desserts. Conversational French lessons and wine classes are offered. Happy hour is from 7 PM–9 PM Mon. through Sat., and Fri. and Sat. nights have live jazz from 7:30 PM–11 PM.

Civello's Raviolismo (214-827-2989; www.civellosraviolismo.com) 1318 North Peak Street, Dallas 75111. Open: Mon. through Fri. 9 AM–3 PM, Sat. by appointment only. Civello's Raviolismo makes fresh pasta by hand daily that is absolutely *delizioso*. They sell four different gourmet lasagnas, Italian sausage, hand-rolled meatballs, fresh tomato sauce, and ravioli with 20-plus filling options. Though the ravioli fillings vary and reflect seasonal changes, some of the fillings include veal with wine-seasoned mushrooms; lump crab meat tossed with fresh basil, green onions, and roasted garlic; feta cheese with black olives and fresh Italian parsley; nutty pumpkin on striped chili pasta; and roasted chili poblano blended in creamy ricotta. Civello's uses fresh, local ingredients and the artisanal cooking techniques of southern Italy and Sicily. What most people don't know is that many of the local restaurants in the DFW area utilize Civello's products in their cuisine, and it is available for diners to incorporate in their own meals. Call the factory to check on daily production and availability of flavors.

Dallas Farmers Market (214-670-5879; www.dallasfarmersmarket.org) 1010 South

There are additional (smaller) farmers' markets in several Metroplex communities: Arlington, Grand Prairie, Coppell, Mansfield, Frisco, McKinney, Fort Worth, Watauga, and Denton.

Pearl Expressway, Dallas 75201. Open: Daily, 8 AM–6 PM, except Thanksgiving Day, Christmas Day, and New Year's Day. Since 1941, The Dallas Farmers Market, located in downtown Dallas, has served as a gathering place for local farmers looking to sell their wares. The Farmers Market is a perfect place for hungry eaters looking for the healthiest and freshest produce, meats, floral, and specialty foods, and connects buyers with high-quality goods that cannot be matched in any grocery store. This one-stop shop is proud to give shoppers a chance to buy local food, much of it grown right here in Texas and within a 150-mile radius of Dallas. There is something going on every day from special events to cooking classes, festivals, culinary demonstrations, and more. A few tips for shoppers: 1) bring cash, as vendors may have limited change, 2) come early for the best selection, 3) arrive late for the best deals, 4) bring your own cloth bag to prevent your purchases from getting bruised, and 5) bring a rolling cart if planning on buying several items—produce is heavy.

Dude, Sweet Chocolate (214-943-5943; www.dudesweetchocolate.com) 408 West Eighth Street, Suite 102, Dallas 75208. Open: Tues. through Thurs. 10 AM–9 PM, Fri. and Sat. 10 AM–10 PM, Sun. 12 PM–5 PM. Named best chocolatier by *D Magazine*, Dude, Sweet Chocolate is a exquisite boutique chocolate shop in the heart of the Bishop Arts District. Unlike many chocolatiers in the Metroplex, they don't offer an overwhelming variety of products, but what

Inside the Dallas Farmers Market. Monica Prochnow

Dude, Sweet Chocolate. Monica Prochnow

they do have is tasty, sophisticated, and beautifully made. Dude offers complex chocolates prepared in-house such as unusual sounding but delicious Fungus Amongus, made with toffee, porcini mush-

rooms, and pumpkin seeds that is an appropriate mix of savory and sweet. The homemade cocoa-puff-flavored marshmallows are densely flavored but covered in powdered sugar for an airy feel, and they are softer than any pillow—just heavenly! They also have fresh ice cream and even sell their goodies to local restaurants for their dessert menus. Their website, unfortunately, is lackluster, and this place requires an in-person visit; but that's okay because they are generous with their samples, and who would dare refuse free chocolate?

Empire Baking Company (214-350-0547; www.empirebaking.com) 5450 West Lovers Lane, Dallas 75209. The Empire Baking Company is an artisanal bakery proudly baking and serving delicious European-style breads and treats. Enter the bakery, and you'll find yourself surrounded by warm and aromatic delights including baguettes, kalamata olive round, jalapeño cheese round, raisin pumpernickel, raisin pecan, walnut scallion round, and challah

Ham Orchards Monica Prochnow

bread, as well as chocolate chip macadamia nut cookies, Danish, rugula, and scones. To ensure the quality and longevity of their bread and treats long after you leave the bakery, the staff is committed to making everything from scratch, even the goodies on their lunch menu. Their apple-smoked bacon, lettuce and roma tomato on the jalapeño cheese bread is to die for. The Dallas-made mozzarella with basil pesto and roma tomato on kalamata olive bread is also recommended. Empire has good salads, too, but why would you order them while in a bakery?

Ham Orchards (972-524-2028; www.ham orchard.com) 11939 County Road 309. Terrell 75161. The fruit around here is just peachy. No, seriously; it really is peachy. This small peach orchard just 40 minutes east of Dallas has been growing 41 varieties of peaches, as well as blackberries, nectarines, strawberries, plums, and plumcots, for more than 30 years. Ham Orchards also sells fresh cucumbers, okra, onions, potatoes, squash, tomatoes, and zucchini. All the produce, whether fruits or vegetables, sold at Ham Orchards is grown locally and are guaranteed to be fresh. In the store, visitors can choose freshly picked or delivered produce selected by the farmers themselves to ensure quality. Inside the store are also selections of butters, cobbler, sauces, dressings, jams, jellies, preserves, fried pies, bread, and pies. Ham Orchards also produces peach and strawberry ice cream—favorites during the dog days of summer during the height of peach season. Visit the pavilion behind the store for hot dogs, hamburgers, and snacks, complete with picnic tables, benches, and rocking chairs for backyard-style dining.

Highland Park Pharmacy Inc. (214-521-2126) 3229 Knox Street, Dallas 75205. Open: Mon. through Sat. 8 AM–6 PM, Sun. 11 AM–6 PM. Feel like a kid again, or at least feel like you're sitting on the set of *Grease* or *Happy Days*. The Highland Park Pharmacy sells plenty of over-the-counter and pre-scription-required products in its pharmacy department, but where it comes alive is as a slice of Americana, complete with old-time soda fountain and lunch counter. This place has been a Dallas tradition since 1912 and has managed to survive the invasion of high-end restaurants that surround it. They have a large counter with plenty of chairs, or you can sit by the window on stools or at tables. Order a milk shake (butterscotch is top-notch), malted, ice cream, or a root beer float from the soda jerk, or stay long enough for a bite from their simple but classic menu. The grilled pimento cheese sandwich is legendary and goes well with limeade. Also try the delicious homemade chicken salad, grilled peanut butter and jelly sandwich, chili dog, egg-salad sandwich, or club sandwich. It's a good spot for breakfast, too. This is a great place for the whole family, but don't bother asking for a latte.

Jimmy's Food Store Fine Italian Food & Wine (214-823-6180; www.jimmysfood store.com) 4901 Bryan Street, Dallas 75206. Open: Mon. through Sat. 9 AM–7:30 PM. Jimmy's seems to carry every type of pasta known—the deli is stocked with a wonderful selection of meats and cheeses, particularly hard-to-find items, like Caciocavallo cheese, wild boar sausage, and Italian cookies. Keep walking through the store to find the rows of imported Italian wines (from over 20 regions in Italy) and sodas, as well as oils, dressings, and a full olive selection. Make sure you give yourself enough time to eat at their lunch counter, as they offer a range of sandwiches—muffalettas and paninis and subs—at reasonable prices, mostly around $5–6. Recommended are the meatball and the Cuban (salty, thick ham and creamy sauce) sandwiches, both cheesy and spicy and only $6. They also offer delicious panini and salads to go. Also the store offers free tastings every Saturday afternoon from 11 AM–4 PM. Get there early if you're shopping for dinner, as they close at 7:30. Parking is awful, but the store and food are worth it.

Mozzarella Cheese Company (214-741-4072; www.mozzco.com) 2944 Elm Street, Dallas 75226. Neighborhood: Deep Ellum. Open: Mon. through Fri. 9 AM–5 PM, Sat. 9 AM–3 PM. In the heart of Deep Ellum lies a culinary gem that often goes unnoticed in a small, nondescript storefront hidden behind a large tree. The Mozzarella Company sports far more in its selection than its moniker implies—mozzarella, mascarpone torta, crème fraiche, smoked scamorza, caciotta, goat cheese, feta, blue cheese, and ricotta, just to name a few. The goat cheeses are tangy, soft, and with just the right amount of herbs. The sweet cream cheese with pralines has a wonderful mix of softness and crunchiness, mixed with subtle flavors that are heavenly. Several of the caciotta cheeses listed in the catalog are made with ancho chiles, ranging from mild to medium, and another one with locally grown basil are just two of several items that can only be found here. The staff is generous with its samples and more than happy to help buyers select just the right cheese. The store offers a variety of different classes to help people learn about pairing their cheeses with wine, beer, and chocolate, as well as participating in cheese making, which includes a factory tour.

Scardello Artisan Cheese (214-219-1300; www.scardellocheese.com) 3511 Oak Lawn Avenue, Dallas 75219. Open: Mon. through Thurs. 11 AM–7 PM, Fri. and Sat. 11 AM–8 PM, Sun. 1 PM–6 PM. Scardello Artisan Cheese, a quaint little cheese monger in the Oak Lawn area of Dallas, proudly sells artisan cheeses featuring American and European farmstead cheese, along with a number of Texas cheeses. With about 150 cheeses in its cases, favorites are the Truffle Tremor and

the Parmigiano-Reggiano Scardello also has a Cheese 101 class for only $25, where students are presented with a plate of goodies, including 18 cheeses, honey, nuts, dried apples, dried pineapple, and lemon, as well as tastings of pinot grigio and Riesling to accompany them. They also carry craft beers from around the world that beautifully pair with everything, as well as a fine selection of bread, crackers, meats, and coffees. Sandwiches are served on-site, but the best part of their menu is the picnic baskets available for rent. Baskets come with three artisan cheeses, a sliced baguette, wine, wineglasses, plates, and other goodies that will make any picnic a hit, all without the fuss or cleanup at the end of the day. Inside Scardello, the atmosphere is open, airy, and modern; yet visitors are immediately embraced by the warm aroma of cheese and the glow from rustic candle chandeliers.

The Cake Ball Company (214-559-5788; www.cakeballs.com) 10230 East Northwest Highway, Dallas 75238. Open: Tues. through Fri. 11 AM–5:30 PM, Sat. 11 AM–2 PM, also by appointment during nonbusiness hours. Indulgence and decadence are celebrated at the Cake Ball Company, and the cake ball has taken the local bakery scene by storm recently. A cake ball is a bite-sized piece of cake (about the size of a golf ball), blended with icing, and shaped to form a ball, then dipped in a rich and creamy chocolate coating. The cake balls are moist and rich and come in 11 exotic flavors: birthday cake, brownie, chocolate buzz, lime margarita, sea salt caramel, lemon, strawberry, red velvet, wedding cake, German chocolate, and chocolate toffee. More flavorful than a cupcake and more elegant than a cookie, cake balls have a gorgeous presentation and are perfect for a tasty dessert, weddings, or corporate gifts. Every mouthwatering cake ball, which comes from one of several long-cherished

Delectable treats from the Cake Ball Company.
Courtesy of the Cake Ball Company.

family recipes, is made by hand and baked fresh daily. Stop by to pick up a few from the dessert case, or call ahead for a custom order.

The Soda Gallery (214-946-7632; www .thesodagallery.com) 408 North Bishop Avenue, Suite 101, Dallas 75208. Neighborhood: Bishop Arts. Open: Tues. through Sat. 11 AM–9 PM, Sun. 11 AM–4 PM. The Soda Gallery, located in the Bishop Arts District in the Oak Cliff area of Dallas, is a fun and inviting boutique shop where visitors can purchase their favorite beverage from almost 200 varieties of sodas. The sodas range from nostalgic and hard-to-find, to new age and novelty items from across the globe. Pop open a bottle of Waialua pineapple soda from Hawaii, Dad's Root Beer from Chicago, or Blenheim Ginger Ale from South Carolina. Also on the shelf is French Orangina, Coca-Cola from Amsterdam (which is made with kola nut), Leninade (a humorous Russian take on lemonade), Nesbitt's, Bubble Up, NuGrape, Vernor's

Ginger Ale, Faygo, Ramune (the soda with the marble) from Japan, and even the local favorite, Dublin Dr Pepper made with pure cane sugar. There are more than 30 different varieties of root beer in stock at any given time. Sodas, always sold in glass bottles, can be purchased individually or in a discounted six-pack, which can be mixed with all of your favorite flavors. There is also a candy section in the back half of the store, filled with fun treats from yesteryear including bubblegum cigarettes and cigars. The Soda Gallery also provides online shopping and shipping, though glass bottles must be carefully wrapped and are costly to mail.

Denton

Bayer's Kolonialwaren (940-759-2822) 824 East Division Street, Muenster 76252. Open: Daily at 6 AM. Bayer's Kolonialwaren, located in the small German town of Muenster, north of Denton, is part specialty bakery and part gas station that sells about a dozen types of freshly baked strudel and locally manufactured sausage. The strudel, baked into 18-inch loaves, is a mix of regular fruit flavors like cherry, strawberry,

The Soda Gallery offers a huge selection of hard-to-find beverages and bottles. Monica Prochnow

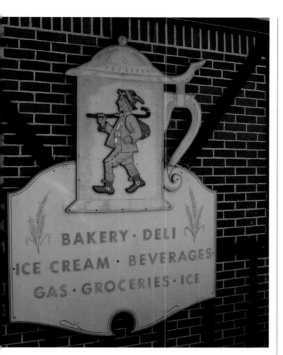

Bayer's Kolonialwaren in Muenster, TX. Monica
Prochnow

apple, blackberry, raspberry, and peach,
and then the same fruit flavors all over
again, but this time with a sweet cream
cheese filler. Bayer's also sells an assortment of locally grown fruit product like
jams and jellies, as well as other freshly
baked treats like doughnuts, specialty
breads (sunflower bread is delicious),
cookies, and sausage kolaches.

Fort Worth

Boudreau Herb Farm (940-325-8674)
5545 Highway 281 North, Mineral Wells
76067. Open: Wed. through Sat. 10 AM–
5 PM. Nothing makes food taste greater than
fresh herbs. Boudreau Herb Farm, a 77-
acre historic and organic farm located just
north of Mineral Wells, Texas, and about an
hour west of Fort Worth, has groves of
native pecans, persimmon, native perenni-
als, antique roses, Mexican plum trees,
mustang grapevines (they grow near the

creek running through the property), wild-
flowers, and an assortment of herbs ripe
for the picking. Inside is an herb store con-
taining teas and products made from herbs
grown on-site, and the greenhouse located
outside has many hard-to-find herb varieties perfect for both cooking and medici-
nal uses.

Curly's Frozen Custard (817-763-8700;
www.curlysfrozencustard.com) 4017 Camp
Bowie Boulevard, Fort Worth 76107. Open:
Sun. through Thurs. 11 AM–10 PM, Fri. and
Sat. 11 AM–11 PM. Curly's menu is ¾ treats
and ¼ eats. Their custard comes in vanilla
(their signature flavor), sugar-free vanilla,
lemon, and chocolate, as well as the flavor/s
of the month, which are always season-
appropriate and vibrantly flavored. They
can be served plain or with any number of
fresh toppings. Can't decide? Choose either
a sundae in fun combinations like peanut
butter fudge, strawberry shortcake, Oreo
brownie deluxe, Snickers fudge, and
bananas foster. Also on the menu are
shakes, malts, and slushes to help wash all
of the sweet goodness down or as a com-
panion to any of their hot dogs, sliders, or
Frito pies. Curly's has a small building and
seating is entirely outside, but it still makes
for a pleasant outing. Drive-through is
available.

Mineral Wells Water Company (940-325-
8870; www.famouswater.com) 209 Northwest Sixth Street, Mineral Wells 76007.
Open: Tues. through Fri. 8 AM–5:30 PM, Sat.
9 AM–5 PM. In the late 19th century, various
areas throughout the state of Texas were
known for its mineral water resorts,
including the city of Mineral Wells, and
were highly sought after for the natural
waters' healthful, curative benefits. For
more than 100 years, the Famous Mineral
Water Company has served the health-
conscious; it is particularly known for water
from its most famous well, the Crazy Well.
This well earned its named from an older

Curly's Frozen Custard on Camp Bowie in Fort Worth. Monica Prochnow

woman who suffered from dementia and drank the water. It was reported to have restorative effects on the "crazy lady's" illness, and the well was dubbed the Crazy Well. The overall popularity of mineral water consumption declined in the 1950s, but Mineral Wells crazy water has had a recent resurgence with greater awareness of health. Water can be purchased at the pavilion, where customers may bring their own containers and have them filled or purchase already-bottled waters right off the shelf. Containers of all sizes are available for sale: 5-gallon, 3-gallon, 1-gallon, 1-liter, .5-liter, and 750-ml glass bottles. Mineral Wells Water Company also sells beauty and health products made from the water, including soaps, body scrubs, linen sprays, lotions, bath oils, and facial toner.

Pendery's Spices (817-924-3434; www.penderys.com) 1407 Eighth Avenue, Fort Worth 76104. Open: Mon. through Fri. 8:30 AM–5 PM, Sat. 9 AM–3 PM. Pendery's touts itself as being a world of chile and spices, but that slogan seems to sell itself short. Located inside a converted home near downtown Fort Worth, Pendery's has an overwhelming selection of goods from all over the globe that are so fresh that they take on entirely new flavors. The company has whole and diced chiles, chile blends, jalapeños, red peppers, paprika, and ristras

Pendery's Spices. Monica Prochnow

for those who adore a little, or in some cases, a big kick in their grub. The spices range from simple to sophisticated and include blends, rubs, and vegetables. Even hard-to-find and luxury items such as saffron can be found at a bargain price. There are also jams, jellies, nuts, sauces, salsas, edible flowers, and an array of gift basket items in-store to choose from. If it belongs in the kitchen or on the grill, Pendery's has it. Our recommendation? If you're a serious chef, go online to the website and download its catalog (80 actual pages, but only 40 when scanned) to avoid the mental overload. Online ordering is also available, but there's nothing like taking in the scents in person. Know that the phone order hours and the storefront hours vary depending on the season, so call before heading over. Wholesale pricing is also available.

Plano

Bailey's Berry Patch (903-564-6228; www.txberry.com) 905 Crawford Road, Sadler 76264. Bailey's Berry Patch is a great place to spend time with the whole family. Come to pick your own fresh berries and enjoy a picnic in a country setting. Bailey's is about an hour and a half north of Dallas, located halfway between Gainesville and Sherman. The Berry Patch has six acres of blueberries, with four varieties to choose from, and three acres of blackberries, also with four varieties. Visitors can pick berries to their heart's content for only $14 for a one-gallon bucket and $5 for a quart-sized bucket. The farm provides everything needed to pick berries, though it is recommended that visitors bring ice coolers to keep their goodies cool during the warmer months. Bailey's also makes numerous blueberry and blackberry foods, like butters, dips, salad dressing, salsas, syrups, and preserves that can be purchased and enjoyed later. There are picnic tables on location, and children are welcome to feed the catfish in the pond. The one disap-

pointment is that Bailey's is not a place to go when feeling spontaneous; visitors must call ahead or sign up on the website to make reservations for a visit, though the limited number of people on-site makes for a relaxing countryside visit.

Henry's Homemade Ice Cream (972-612-9949; www.henryshomemadeicecream .com) 2909 West 15th Street, Plano 75075. Henry's has the standard vanilla, chocolate, and strawberry flavors, which are packed full of creamy richness and flavor, but where this place sparkles is in its unique flavors. The green tea is tangy, the cinnamon is cozy, and the wedding cake is festive. The praline, spumoni, and chocolate-chocolate chip ice creams are also outstanding. Henry's also features seasonal flavors that will leave you sad they aren't available year-round. Henry's has more than just ice cream in a cone; they serve freshly made sorbet and even have ice cream cakes available for taking home, to the hotel room, or to an event.

Hirsch's Meat Market (972-633-5593; www.hirschsmeats.com/index.htm) 1301 West Parker Road, Suite 100, Plano 75023. Open: Tues. through Sat. 10 AM–6 PM. Texans love meat, and Hirsch's Meat Market is more than happy to feed that demand. Hirsch's, it should be noted, does not have bargain meat, but far higher-quality products than what can be found in chain grocery stores. Translation: high-quality meats at loftier pricing. The meat case contains buffalo, venison, rabbit, quail, salmon, tilapia, sea scallops, cod, orange roughy, raw shrimp, cooked shrimp, crab dip, veal shanks, and sausage. If what you want isn't displayed, they usually have what you need in the back, and if you call ahead, they're happy to either obtain it or custom-butcher it for you. The shop is owned and operated by the Hirsch family, and the staff is extremely knowledgeable and more than happy to take the time to show off the different kinds of meats, explain the basic cuts, and offer instruction on how to prepare them. If that weren't enough, Hirsch's sells a variety of woods for enhancing your cooking on the grill—sweet maple, alder, grapevine, peach, pear, apple, cherry, oak, pecan, hickory, mesquite sweetwood blend, and sassafras are available in both chunks and chips and are kiln dried. It is easy to pass this inconspicuous building in an area abundant in strip malls, and parking is limited.

Main Street Bakery and Bistro (972-309-0404; www.themainbakery.com) 7200 Bishop Road, Suite D-11, Plano 75024. Located in the Shops at Legacy, the Main Street Bakery and Bistro is a must-stop shop when perusing the mall. Main Street specializes in handcrafted breads, pastries, and gourmet French and European cuisine for breakfast, lunch, and dinner in a reasonably priced, low-key environment. The extensive menu can be a bit overwhelming, but the staff is friendly and happy to help you sort through it all. For breakfast, have the banana-nut crepes with a side of eggs, their New Orleans–style beignets, or the eggs Benedict. Try the vegetarian-friendly portobello mushroom burger with spinach and avocado stuffing, the warm goat cheese salad, or the tomato and mozzarella panini, which will leave you craving it again. Main Street has free Wi-Fi, great for someone wanting to get some work done but have a cup of coffee and a chocolate éclair while doing it. There are two other locations in DFW: one in Grapevine and the other in Richardson. Voted "Best Neighborhood Restaurant" by *D Magazine* and "Best Croissant in DFW" by *Dallas Morning News*.

NOKA Chocolates (972-527-0801; www.nokachocolate.com) 2040 West Spring Creek Parkway, Plano 75023. Open: Mon. through Sat. 10 AM–9 PM, Sun. 12 PM–6 PM. NOKA Chocolates, located in NorthPark Center between Neiman Marcus and Tiffany & Co., is passionate about its chocolate. Using only the rarest and purest form of chocolate, unadulterated by vanilla and emulsifiers such as soy lecithin, each chocolate candy is hand-crafted from single-estate chocolate, meaning that even the cocoa beans themselves are not mixed. This is a technique used by some of the finest wineries when deciding flavor profiles from grape selections—noting differences in soil and climate—and NOKA treats its chocolates with an equally discriminating hand. The result of this rigidity? Each Vivienté truffle, for example, is made from the finest Venezuelan dark chocolate, using a minimum of 75 percent cacao, from the luxurious ganache center to the delicate outer shell and delicate shavings that decorate the exterior—only pure Venezuelan dark chocolate is used. All of the chocolates are gluten-free, soy-free, do not contain nuts, and are made from fresh cream. Select items are sold in a handful of Neiman Marcus stores in the United States, by Harrods in London, and a few upscale retailers in Taipei and Russia, but the traditional storefront with a full selection is a rarity and can only be found in Dallas and Tokyo, Japan.

Zagat Survey ranked the French Room at the Adolphus the No. 1 restaurant in the United States (2006), as it wrote, "there aren't enough superlatives" to describe it.

The Dallas Farmers Market is the largest working farmers' market in the United States, with more than 1 million visitors annually.

The world's first frozen margarita machine was invented on May 11, 1971 by Dallas restaurateur Mariano Martinez.

Chocolates can be shipped domestically and internationally.

NIGHTLIFE LISTINGS

This is certainly not a comprehensive list of every bar and nightclub in the DFW area, but it should be more than enough to get you started.

Arlington

Blackfinn (817-468-3332; www.blackfinn dallas.com) In the Arlington Highlands, 4001 Bagpiper Way, Suite 101, Arlington 76018. *The* social spot to see and be seen for the under-30 crowd after 10 PM; second location in Addison.

Cowboy's Dancehall (817-265-1535; www .cowboysdancehall.com) 2540 East Abram Street, Arlington 76010. Live country music venue and dance hall; second location in Dallas.

Fox & Hound (817-277-3591; www.foxand hound.com) 1001 Northeast Green Oaks Boulevard, Arlington 76006. A great hangout for after Texas Rangers and Dallas Cowboys games; Additional DFW locations in Lewisville, Fort Worth (two) and Dallas (three).

Improv Comedy Club (817-635-5555; www.improv.com) In the Arlington Highlands, 309 Curtis Mathes Way #147, Arlington 76018. National headliners and household names; connected to Dos Pianos restaurant/piano bar; second Improv location in Addison.

J. Gilligan's (817-274-8561; www.jgilligans .com) 400 East Abram, Arlington 76010. *The* place to hang out before or after a Dallas Cowboys game (shuttle deal offered for all events and games at Cowboys Stadium); live music a couple nights a month.

No Frills Grill & Sports Bar (817-478-1766; www.nofrillsgrill.com) 914 Little Road, Arlington 76017. Exactly what it says it is, but a fun place to hang out and watch a game on big screens with cheap beer; three additional DFW locations: Mansfield, Fort Worth, and Keller.

Sherlock's Baker St. Pub & Grill (817-226-2300; www.sherlockspubco.com) 254 Lincoln Square, Arlington 76011. Live music, reasonable prices, good hangout if you get there early enough to get a seat; Additional DFW locations in Addison, Dallas, and Fort Worth (Baker St. Pub & Grill).

Splitsville (817-465-2695; www.splitsville lanes.com) In the Arlington Highlands, 401 Curtis Mathes Way, Arlington 76018. Restaurant/bowling alley by day; over-21 club/bar (with dress code enforced) after 8 PM; second location in Fairview.

Dallas

Barcadia (214-821-7300; www.barcadia dallas.com) 1917 North Henderson Avenue, Dallas 75206. Fun bar with tons of vintage arcade games and a full menu; *Quick* magazine calls it "the cool kids' version of Dave & Buster's."

Deep Ellum

Just east of downtown Dallas, along Elm Street, Main Street and Commerce Street, north of Exposition Park and south of Bryan Place. With several bars, clubs and live music venues along these three blocks, you're sure to find something for everyone.

Deep Ellum's cutting-edge entertainment, dining and shopping are often compared to New York's SoHo. Formerly an industrial district, Deep Ellum has developed into a popular avant-garde destination. Dallas CVB/Courtesy of the Deep Ellum Association

Deux (214-484-3537; www.deuxlounge .com) at Mockingbird Station, 5321 East Mockingbird Lane #240, Dallas 85206. Luxurious chandeliers and water walls; fashionable crowd; pricey.

Fat Daddy's (972-891-2263; www.fatdaddys dallas.com) 11345 Emerald Street, Dallas 75229. The only all-ages live rock music venue in DFW.

Ghostbar (214-397-4100) at the W Hotel in Victory Park, 2440 Victory Park Lane, Dallas 75219. An artsy rooftop-lounge copycat of the Vegas original.

Insider tip: Women are never charged for entry unless it is a special event, and men are granted complimentary admission on Wednesdays; although Ghostbar is open until 2 AM, they will not allow entry after 12:30 AM.

Glass Cactus Nightclub (817-778-2800; www.gaylordhotels.com/gaylord-texan) at the Gaylord Texan Hotel, 1501 Gaylord Trail, Grapevine 76051. Beautiful spot for a nightcap and fun with a group of friends; a local favorite.

Lakewood Landing (214-823-2410; www .lakewood-landing.com) 5818 Live Oak, Dallas 75214. The ultimate Dallas dive; affordable and chill.

Lee Harvey's (214-428-1555; www.lee harveys.com) 1807 Gould Street, Dallas 75215. Regular live music, best jukebox in town, unpretentious, large outdoor area, dogs welcome.

McKinney Ave. Tavern (214-969-1984; www.thematonline.com) 2822 McKinney Avenue, Dallas 75204. Always a fun hang-out; co-owned by local radio personality Big Al from the nationally syndicated *Kidd Kraddick in the Morning* show—Big Al is notorious for taking over the mic to rev up the crowd at inopportune times . . . such as during the Super Bowl.

Primo's (214-220-0510; www.primos dallas.com) 3309 McKinney Avenue, Dallas 75204. Award-winning Tex-Mex and a favorite late-night watering hole for locals, including chefs and those in hospitality; second location in Garland.

The Granada (214-824-9933; www.granada theater.com) 3524 Greenville Avenue, Dallas 75206. Legendary live music venue; football-watching parties on the big screens.

The Libertine Bar (214-824-7900; www .libertinebar.com) 2101 Greenville Avenue, Dallas 75206. Voted "Best Bar, Period." by the *Dallas Observer* for 2008.

The Palladium Ballroom (214-421-2021; www.thepalladiumballroom.com) 1135 South Lamar Street, Dallas 75215. Not fancy, but a very open live music venue that makes for an intimate concert experience; drinks surprisingly affordable.

Urban Oasis Lounge (214-468-8397; www.hotelzazadallas.com/dallas-tx-lounges .php) at Hotel ZaZa, 2332 Leonard Street, Dallas 75201. Trendy, young, and fashion- able with a pool through the middle and views of the Uptown Dallas skyline.

Denton

Cool Beans (940-382-7025) 1210 West Hickory Street, Denton 76201. A textbook "college bar"—laid-back and grungy.

Dan's Silverleaf (940-320-2000; www .danssilverleaf.com) 103 Industrial Street, Denton 76201. Best live music venue in Denton.

Denton Side Bar (940-382-4139; www .dentonsidebar.com) 109 Avenue A, Denton 76201. A little sports bar with cheap booze, video games, and plasma TVs.

Hailey's (940-323-1159; www.haileysclub .com) 122 West Mulberry Street, Denton 76201. Great live music venue with an extensive beer selection.

Rockin Rodeo (940-565-6611; www.rock inrodeodenton.com) 1003 Avenue C, Denton 76201. Primarily a country music venue; Randy Rogers, Charlie Robison, Stoney LaRue, The Eli Young Band, and Texas-country favorite Brandon Rhyder have all graced its stage.

The Loophole (940-565-0770; www.loop holepub.com) 119 West Hickory Street, Denton 76201. Fun atmosphere, located on the historic downtown square.

Two Charlies Bar & Grill (940-891-1100; www.twocharlies.com) 809 Sunset Street, Denton 76201. Simple and casual; as classy as Denton bars come.

Fort Worth

7th Haven (817-744-8550) 2700 West Seventh Street, Fort Worth 76107. Rooftop patio with affordable drinks and a laid- back crowd.

8.0 Bar (817-336-0880; www.eightobar .com) 111 East Third Street, Fort Worth 76102. Huge patio, live music, full menu.

Billy Bob's Texas (817-624-7117; www .billybobstexas.com) 2520 Rodeo Plaza, Fort Worth 76164. The world's largest honky-tonk; historic music venue in the Fort Worth Stockyards (see recreation chapter for more information).

Hyena's Comedy Club (817-877-5233; www.hyenascomedynightclub.com) 605 Houston Street, Fort Worth 76102. Great venue to see not-so-famous comedians and local talent; two-drink minimum; addi- tional locations in Dallas and Arlington.

Pete's Dueling Piano Bar (817-335-7383; www.petesduelingpianobar.com) 621 Houston Street, Fort Worth 76102. High-energy classics from CCR, Steve Miller Band, and, of course, Billy Joel; be prepared to sing along; second location in Addison.

Rahr & Sons Brewery (817-810-9266; www.rahrbrewing.com) 701 Galveston Avenue, Fort Worth 76104. Tour/tasting events Wednesdays and Saturdays.

The Flying Saucer Draught Emporium (817-336-7470; www.beerknurd.com) 111 East Fourth Street, Fort Worth 76102. More than 240 beers and a great patio area; second location in Addison.

The Ginger Man (817-886-2327; www.ftworth.gingermanpub.com) 3716 Camp Bowie Boulevard, Fort Worth 76107. Excellent beer selection and great food; additional locations in Dallas and Plano.

The Pour House (817-335-2575; www.pourhousefw.com) 2725 West Seventh Street, Fort Worth 76107. Doesn't take itself too seriously; a local favorite with college kids and the under-30 crowd.

White Elephant Saloon (817-624-8273; www.whiteelephantsaloon.com) 106 East Exchange Avenue, Fort Worth 76102. A fun hangout with a history almost as old as Fort Worth itself.

Plano

Fox Sports Grill (972-312-1369; www.foxsportsgrill.com/plano) at The Shops at Legacy, 5741 Legacy Drive, Plano 75024. One of only six locations in the country; good happy hour specials.

The Flying Saucer Draught Emporium. Monica Prochnow

Billy Bob's Texas. Fort Worth CVB

The Endzone Sports Bar & Grill (972-867-3400; www.endzonesportsbarand grill.com) 3033 West Parker Road #109, Plano 75023. Great for sports-watching, of course; friendly staff; nongame nights may have karaoke, poker tournaments, or a live DJ.

The Fillmore Pub (972-423-2400; www .thefillmorepub.com) 1004 East Fifteenth Street, Plano 75074. Cozy, with a great beer selection and very affordable full menu; second location in McKinney.

The Holy Grail Pub (972-377-6633; www .theholygrailpub.com) 8240 Preston Road, Plano 75024. Relaxed atmosphere, but these servers seriously know their beers; above and beyond a typical pub menu— amazing and amazingly inexpensive.

6

Sports

Hometown Heroes

The DFW area is the southwest's only metro area to host teams from five major professional sports leagues: NFL, MLB, NBA, NHL, and MLS. Football in Texas could be its own
religion (enough movies and TV shows have been made about Texas teams to prove we're
obsessed). The area's passion for sports runs wide and deep, no doubt, and even extends to
the area's minor-league teams, collegiate teams, and even high school football. With all the
season overlap, there is sure to be a sporting event going on almost any time of the year.

PROFESSIONAL SPORTS

Football

Dallas Cowboys (www.dallascowboys.com) The Dallas Cowboys as a team were born in
January 1960. Originally labeled as the Rangers and brought in as an expansion team, the
team eventually was renamed the Cowboys. The other Dallas football team, the Dallas
Texans, moved to Missouri and were transformed into the Kansas City Chiefs, leaving the
Cowboys to take over as Texas's only pro football team.

Also referred to as "America's Team," the Dallas Cowboys are one of the most recognizable sports franchises in the world—and also one of the most successful teams in the history
of the National Football League, boasting five Super Bowl Championships (1972, 1978,
1993, 1994, and 1996).

The team's highly anticipated new stadium opened in 2009, dubbed "The Palace in
Dallas" by national media (which sparked an uproar from DFW residents noting "the
Palace" is actually in Arlington), is the largest domed stadium in the world, has the world's
largest column-free interior and the largest high-def video screen, which hangs from 20-
yard line to 20-yard line. It is first-class all the way. The retractable-roof stadium has can
seat almost 100,000 fans (110,000 maximum capacity, including standing-room areas),
ranking as the third largest stadium in the NFL by seating capacity. The "Party Pass" sections are behind the seats in each end zone and on a series of six elevated platforms connected by stairways—Party Pass tickets are much more inexpensive than an actual ticket for

LEFT: *The Texas Rangers played in their first-ever World Series in 2010.* T| Moye

a seat. For information on stadium tours, please see the recreation chapter. Please note: game-day parking is quite pricey, but there are several Arlington hotels (see lodging chapter) and shopping centers, like Lincoln Square (see shopping chapter) that offer complimentary or low-cost shuttle service to and from the stadium.

Dallas Vigilantes (www.dallasvigilantes .com) Dallas Cowboys games are not always accessible for everyone due to the cost, the traffic, and the crowds, which leads us to the Dallas Vigilantes, the Arena Football League's team for the DFW area. To get your football fix during the spring and summer without all the drama, see the Vigilantes at Dallas's American Airlines Center (AAC); the season runs Apr. through July.

Baseball

Texas Rangers (texas.rangers.mlb.com) After Dallas lobbied the American League for a baseball team for years, the

The Cowboys' first season to play in their new Arlington stadium was 2009–2010 and already the stadium has already played host to North Texas' first Super Bowl ever, Super Bowl XLV, February 6, 2011. The Cowboys' previous home, Texas Stadium in Irving, was never considered suitable because its roof wasn't closeable.

It has always been said that the reason for the hole on top of the stadium is so that God can watch his favorite team play (both Texas Stadium and Cowboys Stadium had/have giant holes in the roof).

The Texas Rangers played in their first-ever World Series in 2010. T| Moye

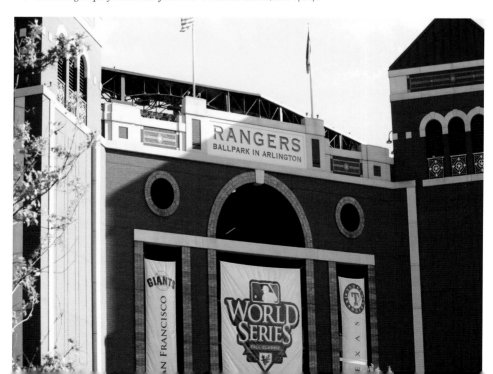

Taking in a minor-league Fort Worth Cats baseball game is major-league fun. Laura Heymann

Washington Senators were moved from Washington, D.C., to Arlington, Texas in 1972 and were renamed the Texas Rangers. Attending Rangers games at the Ballpark in Arlington is a very popular pastime April through October in DFW. The Ballpark seats about 50,000 fans and you should try to wear red, whit,e or blue to a game. Fans should also know the popular team phrases "Antlers up!" (when a Ranger steals a base, i.e., runs fast like a deer) and "The Claw" (the players raise the claw to each other when a good offensive play is made).

Fort Worth Cats (www.fwcats.com) Baseball came to Fort Worth in 1887 as the Fort Worth Panthers, which eventually became the minor-league Fort Worth Cats, and the team won an unprecedented six consecutive championships from 1920 to 1925. The Cats play at historic LaGrave Field off Main Street, near the Stockyards in Fort Worth. Many famous names in baseball have graced historic LaGrave Field, from Babe Ruth to Willie Mays. The field includes a kid zone with bounce houses and other attractions for little ones, as well as several concession

The Ballpark hosted the 1995 MLB All-Star Game.

Former Texas Rangers pitcher Nolan Ryan purchased the team in 2010.

The Rangers won their first-ever ALCS Championship in 2010 against the New York Yankees and appeared in their first-ever World Series as well, though they ultimately lost to the San Francisco Giants.

options. The Cats' mascot, a large black cat named Dodger, always comes out to rev up the crowd around the second or third innings and makes continued appearances throughout the game, much to the crowd's delight.

Insider tip: Friday night games feature a great fireworks show set to music, and children are allowed on the field to run the bases after the game as well.

Grand Prairie AirHogs (www.airhogs baseball.com) The Grand Prairie AirHogs are another minor-league baseball team in the area. The AirHogs play at QuickTrip Park in the heart of Grand Prairie's entertainment district, directly between Lone Star Park and Verizon Theatre. Amenities at the stadium include a pool and party deck, a 17,000-square-foot playground,

Insider tip: Park in the south parking lot, as pop flies can come dangerously close to hitting cars in the lot immediately surrounding the field.

third-base party deck, Outfield Cigar Bar, and several concession options; parking is free.

The name "AirHogs" is a slang term used by U.S. military pilots and refers to Grand Prairie's aviation industry.

Frisco RoughRiders (web.minorleaguebaseball.com/index.jsp?sid=t540) The Frisco RoughRiders are currently the Class AA affiliate of the Texas Rangers. They currently play at the Dr Pepper Ballpark in Frisco, just across the street from IKEA. Opened in 2003, the stadium seats more than 10,000 fans, and there is even a pool area available for rental just beyond the right center field wall.

Basketball

Dallas Mavericks (www.nba.com/mavericks) Founded in 1980, the Mavericks have become one of the NBA's most exciting franchises, especially after being crowned Western Conference Champions in 2005–2006. Join the very animated team owner Mark Cuban at the state-of-the-art AAC October through April to see the Mavs square off against the NBA's best.

Hockey

Dallas Stars (stars.nhl.com) It may be surprising to some that DFW has such a large hockey following, since we are in one of the hottest areas of the country, but the 1999 Stanley Cup Champion Dallas

The 2007 NHL All-Star Game was played at Dallas's AAC.

Stars have always been a very hot ticket. Watch them face off against the best of the NHL September through April at the AAC in Dallas.

Soccer

FC Dallas (www.fcdallas.com) Winners of the 1997 U.S. Open Cup, FC Dallas (formerly the Dallas Burn) is the area's only Major League Soccer franchise. They play Apr. through Oct. at Pizza Hut Park in Frisco.

Texas Motor Speedway. Robert Laberge/Getty Images for Texas Motor Speedway

NASCAR (www.texasmotorspeedway .com) Recognized as one of the most modern speedways in the world, Texas Motor Speedway (TMS) has an event nearly every day of the year. The super-speedway is one of the largest sports and entertainment facilities in America. The state-of-the-art complex hosts the NASCAR Sprint Cup, Nationwide Series and Craftsman Truck Series as well as the Indy Car Series each year.

Golf (www.hpbnc.org/byronnelson) The HP Byron Nelson Championship is held in honor of Byron Nelson, whose incredible winning streak and scoring average earned him the honor of being the first professional golfer to have a PGA TOUR event created in his name. The event is held each spring at the TPC Four Seasons Dallas at Las Colinas. The course's 2008 multimillion-dollar renovation was specifically designed to challenge the professional golfer as well as entertain today's savvy amateurs. The renovation features an upgraded pavilion, a dynamic new area for kids and families, and even better golf viewing on every hole.

Since his passing in 2006, players of FC Dallas have worn a patch with a Circle LH to honor the legacy of Lamar Hunt, the man who brought professional soccer to the United States.

Insider tip: TMS traffic can be extremely difficult to navigate on a race day; many NASCAR fans arrive days ahead of time in RV campers.

Texas Motor Speedway. Fort Worth CVB

An excited crowd at a Dallas Mavericks basketball game. Dallas CVB/American Airlines Center

COLLEGIATE SPORTS

TCU (gofrogs.cstv.com) The area's college football team with the largest following and fan base, by far, is the Texas Christian University Horned Frogs. Members of the Mountain West Conference, the Frogs have won two national championships and 15 conference championships in five different conferences. Additionally, the program has had legendary players including Bob Lilly, Sammy Baugh, Davey O'Brien, and LaDainian Tomlinson. The Frogs play at the Amon G. Carter stadium on the TCU campus in Fort Worth. The stadium opened in 1930 and holds about 44,000 fans, mostly dressed in a sea of purple. But in 2009, TCU posted on its official Twitter page that the night's game against Utah "broke the attendance record in Amon Carter Stadium with 50,307." The Frogs remained undefeated in both their 2009 and 2010 regular seasons and won the Rose Bowl 21-19 New Year's Day 2011, surprising everyone, especially university football giant Wisconsin and proponents of the BCS.

HIGH SCHOOL FOOTBALL

Southlake Carroll Dragons (www.carrolldragons.org) High school athletics in Texas should not be considered child's play, and the hit TV show *Friday Night Lights* (based on a Texas high school football team) proves it. One local favorite, the Southlake Carroll Dragons, has won 36 state titles since 1975 (including football, wrestling, golf, cross country, swimming, baseball, soccer, basketball, marching band, one-act play, academic champion, robotics, accounting, and computer science). Carroll also won the Lone Star Cup in the 2000–2001 and 2001–2002 school years as a 4A school and in the 2003–2004 school year as a 5A school (the class featuring the state's largest high schools).

Texas Motor Speedway. Darrell Ingham/Getty Images

The Dragons are recognized nationwide, in large part because of their extremely successful football program; they have won five state championships in recent years. Several of their games have been televised nationally, and the team has played on Cowboys turf in multiple playoff and championship games.

Trinity Trojans (in Euless) (www.trinity trojanfootball.com) The Class 5A Trinity Trojan football team is constantly in the national spotlight due to its rich football history, including three state titles in recent years. The 2008 football season brought a great deal of national attention, during which Rivals.com ranked the Trojans No. 1 in the nation.

Over the years, the football team has earned 23 Texas State Playoff appearances, including 20 District Championships, seven semifinal appearances, five state championship appearances, and three state titles. Trinity played the first high school football game at the new Cowboys Stadium in 2009. Trinity went on to defeat many teams that season, including an 88–27 win against Flower Mound, marking the largest number of points scored in a high school football game since 1941.

The FC Dallas Major League Soccer team played its home games at Southlake Carroll's Dragon Stadium and the Cotton Bowl in Dallas until they got their own stadium, Pizza Hut Park, in Frisco in 2005.

The team is also known for performing the "Ka Mate Haka" an old Māori war dance, which they perform before and after their games. The "Haka" has been featured in various articles and national newscasts around the country.

The Trojans football team was featured in a Gatorade commercial broadcast in 2007 during the FedEx Orange Bowl.

7

RECREATION

If It's Not Fun, You're Not Doing It Right

Texas is the second largest state in terms of population, with over 24 million people. It also has a birth rate of over 405,000 babies born each year. Not only does that mean that Texas needs a strong infrastructure to support the people that live here and its ever-growing population, but there is also a large demand for entertainment and recreation for people in their nonworking or nonschooling hours.

As such, recreation, and just as important, family-friendly activities are essential to the quality of life in Texas, and of course, DFW. Most cities offer a variety of activities within their immediate communities, but in this chapter, you will find a lot of our favorite or unique activities in the Metroplex, almost all of which are family-friendly. Both indoor and outdoor activities are presented here.

CITY TOURS

Dallas Segway Tours (972-821-9054; www.dallassegwaytours.com) 1907 North Lamar Street, Dallas 75202. Tour times vary, costs $50–$70 not including tax or tip

Why walk when you can cruise? The Dallas Segway Tours, which are led by knowledgeable tour guides, give a local's view of Dallas. All riders will be given a 30-minute orientation, a helmet, a bottle of water, and the latest Segway model to cruise around in on one of three possible tours. The first tour is the West End Adventure Tour. This heavily narrated tour is a visit through modern and historic downtown Dallas. Taken at a slow and easy pace, this tour visits the JFK memorial and the infamous grassy knoll, Dealey Plaza, the Dallas Police Memorial, Pioneer Plaza, and Pioneer Cemetery. The Katy Trail Nature Tour is a quiet tour with little narration, and its primary focus is on enjoying the scenery. Riders will glide through Victory Park, traverse the Katy Trail, and finish the excursion with a ride through Reverchon Park. This tour enables nature lovers to gaze upon birds, trees, butterflies, and other earthly delights. The American Airlines Tour is the abbreviated version of the Katy Trail Nature Tour and entails a quick visit to the American Airlines Center and AT&T Plaza. All three tours originate in the lobby of SpringHill Suites in the Dallas West End Historic District.

LEFT: *At the State Fair* Laura Heymann

AT&T Plaza and American Airlines Center. Dallas CVB/American Airlines Center

Horse-Drawn Carriage Tours

In the downtowns of both Fort Worth and Dallas are horse-drawn carriages that will take you on sightseeing tours. Tours, traditional and customized, can range anywhere from 15 minutes to an hour and cost between $30 and $165. Carriages are also available for weddings, engagements, romantic rides, or for simple family fun. Dallas Surrey Services (Dallas), 214-946-9911

Belle Starre Carriages (Dallas), 214-855-0410, www.carriagetours.net) Brazos Carriage (Fort Worth), 817-723-2322, www.brazoscarriage.com/historictour.htm.

Classic Carriages (Fort Worth), 817-336-0400, www.classiccarriages.net).

Insider tip: There are some restrictions on participation in the Segway Tour. All riders must meet all safety requirements before being permitted to operate a Segway: open-toed shoes and high heels are prohibited. Riders must be at least 14 years old, and youth between 14 and 17 must have a signed waiver of consent from a parent or legal guardian. Riders must weigh between 100 and 260 pounds, and pregnant women cannot ride under any circumstances.

Sightseeing Bus Tours

For large groups of people, chartering a bus might be an ideal way to sightsee. Costs vary depending on the destination and the number of people.

Coach America DFW, 1-800-256-4723 or 214-988-3000, www.grayline.com)
Eagle Tours, Inc., 972-721-0545, www.eagletoursinc.com)
Heritage Tours, LLC, 214-265-7782, www.heritagetoursllc.com)
All In One Tour Services, 214-698-0332, www.allinonetourservices.com)

WALKING AROUND

Arlington

Arlington Entertainment District Road to Six Flags, Arlington 76012. Arlington's entertainment district is in the northern part of the city, bounded by I-30 on the north, SH 360 on the east, Division Street to the south, and Center Street to the west. Within this area are several major attractions: Six Flags Over Texas, Hurricane Harbor, Texas Rangers Ballpark, Dallas Cowboys' Stadium, Lincoln Square Shopping Center, and the Arlington Convention Center.

Dallas

Bishop Arts District Bishop Street, Dallas 75208. The Bishop Arts District, which is the area along Bishop Street near Davis Street, is a small but funky former warehouse district in the Oak Cliff area of Dallas. This revitalized and artsy two-block area remains one of Dallas's best-kept secrets and is home to more than 50 local restaurants, boutiques, and services. No chain stores here. Bishop is a walkable, urban environment, though the outlying areas are not as rejuvenated. Bishop is easily accessible, as it is just five minutes south of downtown Dallas. It is also known to be a GLBT-friendly area.

Dallas Arts District Ross Avenue, Dallas 75201. The Dallas Arts District is the largest arts district in the nation, spanning 68 acres and 19 contiguous blocks in downtown Dallas. The district is comprised of museums (Dallas Museum of Art, Nasher Sculpture Center, Trammel Crow Center, Crow Collection of Asian Art) and two performance halls (the Meyerson Symphony Center and the AT&T Performing Arts Center, which also hosts the Winspear Opera House), and the Dallas Black Dance Theatre, with new arts amenities being added all of the time.

Deep Ellum Elm Street, Dallas 75226. Three blocks east of downtown Dallas is Deep Ellum, or an area of Dallas that is deep into Elm (Elm becomes Ellum and said with a drawl, please) Street. It is the stretch along Elm Street that is north of Exposition Park and south of Bryan Place. This former warehouse district is home to an array of unique shops, tattoo parlors, eclectic restaurants, and residential lofts surrounded by numerous blues, jazz, reggae, and alternative rock clubs. There are several public art displays, colorful graffiti, and unusual goings-on that make this an exciting place.

Big Tex greets more than 3 million visitors to the State Fair of Texas each year. The State Fair is held annually at Fair Park, located near Downtown Dallas. Dallas CVB (Courtesy of Fair Park)

DOWNTOWN

Main Street, Dallas 75201. Downtown Dallas, full of beauty and history, is an area growing in nightlife, historic shopping, and luxury hotels. Dine at the Adolphus

Downtown Dallas has loads of great architecture to take in. Frank Goodenough

Hotel's French Room or Charlie Palmer at the Joule, or stay at the historic Magnolia Hotel. Shop at the original Neiman Marcus store—there is plenty to do and see downtown.

Fair Park 1121 First Avenue, Dallas 75210. Fair Park, unlike the other neighborhoods of Dallas, does not include residents; it is the city's largest cultural center and has 277 acres of museums, exhibit facilities, and green park spaces. Included in the area is the 71,000-seat Cotton Bowl, the 130-seat Margo Jones Theater, exquisite examples of Art Deco architecture, and the home of the largest state fair in the nation each September and October. Fair Park is just 2 miles east of downtown.

Greenville Avenue Dallas 75206. Greenville Avenue, specifically the area from Ross Avenue to Lovers Lane, is one of the oldest entertainment areas in Dallas. It is just northeast of downtown and divided into Upper and Lower Greenville Avenue with Mockingbird Lane as the dividing line. Lower Greenville is older, has a greater concentration of bars that are accessible by foot, and lines up next to one of the largest neighborhoods of arts and crafts homes from the early 1900s. They host several local festivals each year including the Greenville Avenue St. Patrick's Day Parade, which is a daylong street party. Upper Greenville has an urban village feel, with a mixture of lofts, restaurants, art house cinemas, shopping, and an occasional bar.

Highland Park Highland Park Village Road, Dallas 75205. Highland Park is a 2.2-square-mile town completely surrounded by the city of Dallas on the south, east, and west and University Park on the north. Highland Park Village is known for its beautiful architecture

At the State Fair Laura Heymann

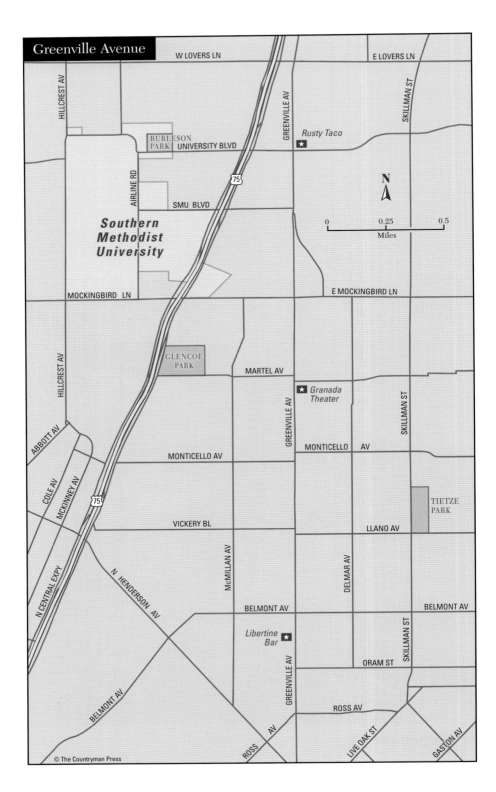

Greenville Avenue

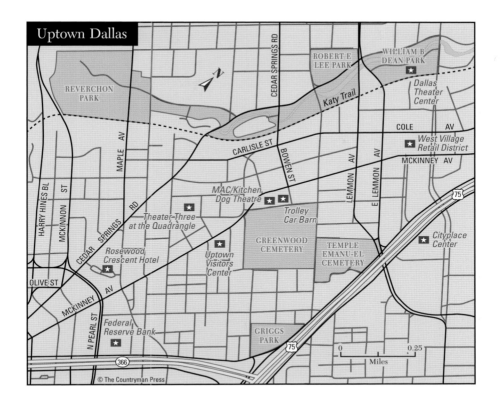

Uptown Dallas

and upscale retailers such as Chanel, Hermès, Carolina Herrera, Tory Burch, Harry Winston, Escada, Ralph Lauren, and Jimmy Choo, among others.

Knox-Henderson Street Dallas 75205. Knox-Henderson is the dual-named street that crosses North Central Expressway near the Southern Methodist University campus. On the west side of the expressway is Knox Street, which is filled with 1920s-area storefronts that house both fashionable stores and adorable boutique shops. Transversely, the east side is Henderson Street, which is home to restaurants, galleries, and antique shops and is the party place for upscale nightclubs and bistros. The area has seen a significant effort, as of late, to preserve its historical richness and appeal.

Oak Lawn Cedar Springs Road, Dallas 75201. For more than 25 years, the Oak Lawn neighborhood has been the epicenter of all the GLBT activities in the city. It is one of the wealthier and artsy areas, with many professionals and urban types living in upscale homes. Cedar Springs Road and Throckmorton Street is where gay activism in Dallas began, and shops, dining, and nightlife have thrived in the area.

Swiss Avenue Historic District Dallas 75204. Some of Dallas's early, wealthy residents lived in huge brick and stone mansions ranging in traditional architectural styles from

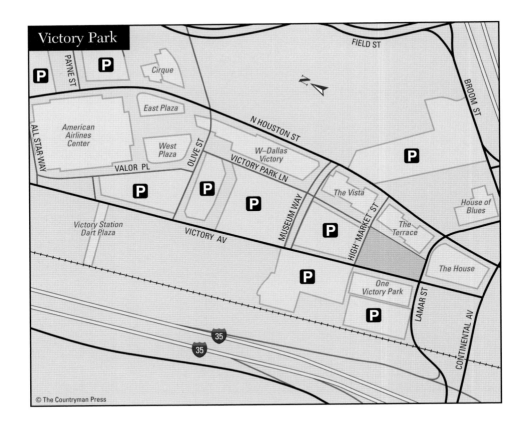

Tudor to Spanish Renaissance to Prairie and art deco. Listed in the National Register of Historic Places, these 200 carefully preserved and restored homes create an area perfect for gazing, either in a casual stroll or an afternoon drive. Swiss Avenue is known to have vibrant light displays and decorations during the holiday season.

Uptown McKinney Avenue, Dallas TX 75204. Northeast of downtown is the 120-year-old-plus neighborhood known as Uptown. The chic area has seen a recent revitalization, and the area includes more than 80 restaurants, one-of-a-kind boutiques, spas, art galleries, upscale shopping, high-end hotels, and bed-and-breakfasts. The M-Line connects Uptown with the Dallas Arts District.

Victory Park Olive Street, Dallas 75219. Victory Park is a 75-acre master-planned area in downtown Dallas, just north of the West End. It is located at the intersection of Interstate 35E, the North Dallas Tollway, and the Woodall Rodgers Freeway. Victory Park is home to the American Airlines Center, Dallas Convention Center, Dallas Market Center, and the Katy Trail.

West End Historic District Munger Avenue, Dallas 75202. The 55-acre West End Historic District, or West End, once an area for warehouses and railroad stations, is the hub of tourism in Dallas, featuring the Sixth Floor Museum, the infamous grassy knoll, and plenty of historical sites. It also has plenty of places to shop, dine, and enjoy live entertainment. Visit "Old Red," the downtown courthouse that is home to the Dallas Tourist Information Center, for information.

A statue depicting a cowboy wrestling a steer in the Fort Worth Stockyards. Monica Prochnow

Denton County Courthouse. Monica Prochnow

West Village McKinney Avenue, Dallas 75204. West Village, rooted in a trendy uptown neighborhood, is a five-block, upscale hot spot with al fresco dining, bars, a bookstore, coffee shop, indie movie theater, and trendy shops where you can stroll along tree-lined village streets while window-shopping and admiring the 1930s-style architecture. Ride free on the M-Line through the area. West Village is located near downtown Dallas and McKinney Avenue between Blackburn Street and Lemmon Avenue.

Fort Worth

Sundance Square Main Street, Fort Worth 76102. Sundance Square in downtown Fort Worth, formerly Hell's Half Acre, was once known for its saloons, gambling parlors, and dance halls. The area is full of beautifully restored buildings, upscale restaurants, and trendy shopping. There are also

More interesting downtown Dallas architecture. Frank Goodenough

live theaters, several museums, art galleries, a movie theater, a comedy club, and a world-class concert and performance hall.

Fort Worth Stockyards National Historic District East Exchange Avenue, Fort Worth 76164. The Fort Worth Stockyards National Historic District, or the Stockyards, is at the intersection of Main Street and East Exchange Avenue. It is the cornerstone of modern Fort Worth history, as the place where cattle were once bought and sold, penned for shipping, and even processed at the famous Swift and Armour meatpacking plants. At the Stockyards are historical sites, western shopping, restaurants, steakhouses, and plenty of live entertainment, as well as lots of cows.

Denton

Denton on the Square Locust Street, Denton 76201. Forming a perimeter around the historic city courthouse that spirals into the sky and is seen from all directions, the Denton on the Square neighborhood extends past the immediate streets that surround it. Denton on the Square is home to restaurants, shopping, theaters, and more.

THINGS TO DO AND SEE

Arlington

Dallas Cowboys Stadium Tour (1-800-745-3000; stadium.dallascowboys.com /tours/tourInfo.cfm) 900 East Randol Mill Road, Arlington 76011. Open: Mon. through Sat. 10 AM–6 PM (last tour at 4:30 PM), Sun. 11 AM–5 PM (last tour at 3:30 PM). Admission: Self-guided tours (adults $17.50, children $14.50), VIP-guided tours (adults $27.50, children and seniors $22.50). Two types of tours are offered at the world's largest domed structure: self-guided and VIP guided tours. The VIP Guided Tour is your best option for touring the entire stadium and being fed facts and figures about America's Team, as well as having the ability to interact with and ask questions of a knowledgeable guide. VIP-guided tours last 60 to 90 minutes; you can walk at your own pace during a self-guided tour.

Six Flags Hurricane Harbor (817-640-8900; www.sixflags.com/hurricane HarborTexas) 1800 East Lamar Boulevard, Arlington 76006. Open: Varies, depending on time of year. Admission: Adults and children 48 inches and taller $25.99, children under 47 inches $19.99, toddlers (0–2) free. Looking for hydro-powered thrills? Look no further, because you've found some of the tallest, fastest, wettest, craziest water rides in the country. From slippery slides to splashy play areas for tots and even a 1-million-gallon wave pool, there is a respite from the crazy Texas heat. Ride the lazy river for relaxation or to get to your next thrill. Parking is $10.

Insider tip: These tours are popular and sell out quickly. Call ahead to reserve tickets or purchase them online prior to your arrival. Tours depart from the Pro Shop located at Entrance A. Parking is free in Lot 1 and Lot 2 off Randol Mill Road.

Six Flags Over Texas (817-640-8900; www.sixflags.com/overTexas) 2201 Road to Six Flags, Arlington 76011. Open: Varies, depending on time of year. Admission: Adults and

Cowboys Stadium in Arlington. Monica Prochnow

children 48 inches or taller $51.99, children under 48 inches $32.99, toddlers (0–2) free. Six Flags Over Texas amusement park offers fun for the entire family with 13 thrilling roller coasters, including Tony Hawk's Big Spin, and a multitude of additional attractions, rides, shows, shops, and eats.

Texas Rangers Ballpark Tour (817-273-5099; texas.rangers.mlb.com/tex/ballpark/tours.jsp) 1000 Ballpark Way, Arlington 76011. Open: Various, depends on game schedule. Admission: Adults $10, seniors (62+), $8, youth (4–18) $5, children (0–4) free. See the most exciting behind-the-scenes areas of this stunning 270-acre ballpark including the Rangers

Insider tip: If you purchase tickets online at either of the Six Flags properties, they are discounted significantly. Also, search online for coupons for additional savings or promotions.

clubhouse, its batting cages, the press box, and the dugouts. All tours start at the First Base Box Office located on the south side of Rangers Ballpark. Look for the Tours window, where tickets may be purchased in advance or at tour time and are subject to availability. Tours are offered year-round, but check the website, as the tour schedule is determined by the game schedule.

Dallas
Dallas Heritage Village (214-428-5448) 1515 South Harwood Street, Dallas 75215. Open: Tues. through Sat. 10 AM–4 PM, Sun. 12 PM–4 PM; closed Jan. and Aug., as well as Thanksgiving, Christmas Eve, Christmas, New Year's Eve, and New Year's Day. Admission: Adults $7, seniors (65+) $5, children (4–12) $4, toddlers (0–2) free. The Dallas Heritage

Village is a living architectural museum. Nestled in 13 wooded acres just south of downtown Dallas, the village allows visitors of all ages and interests to understand Dallas history in a meaningful, hands-on way. The museum is comprised of 38 historic structures and boasts a Civil War–era farm, several elegant Victorian homes, a school, a church, a bank, a newspaper print shop, a saloon, a hardware store, and more. Visitors can stroll through the village at their own pace, guided by pamphlets or by hearing first-person interpretations through their cell phones. Guided tours, which are offered daily at 1:30 pm for free, are also available. Actors dressed in period clothing bring the museum to life, as gunfighters, a wagonmaster, the blacksmiths, or even Mrs. Kennedy, who is a gracious hostess and willing to play checkers with you in her parlor, are eager to welcome you to their town and entertain your questions.

Insider tip: Visitors can take classes at the village: the first is the Village Academy for children ages four to 10, where they learn about local history in an afternoon. The other is a hands-on blacksmithing course for adults or older teens in which visitors learn how to make tools during two four-hour sessions. Reservations for the Village Academy are required one week in advance, and reservations for the blacksmithing course are required four weeks in advance with a $50 nonrefundable deposit at booking.

Dallas Heritage Village Monica Prochnow

Dallas Indoor Rock Climbing (972-231-7625; www.dallasclimbing.com) 9201 Forest Lane, Dallas 75243. Open: Mon. through Fri. 1 PM–10 PM, Sat. 10 PM–9 PM, Sun. 11 AM–5 PM. Admission: Day pass $12 (does not include $3 harness, $3 chalk bag, and $5 shoe rentals), the works pass $21 (includes all equipment), belay class for first-timers $2. Dallas Rocks is part gym and part indoor rock climbing facility. The rock-climbing portion has more than 14,000 square feet of climbing surface. With 14- and 16-foot top-out bouldering and 35-foot route walls, Dallas Rocks is able to accommodate climbers of all ages and ability levels. If you're feeling adventurous, try their Big Tex bouldering wall with 35 linear feet of sustained 70- and 45-degree overhang or their cave with 120 linear feet of 70-degree overhang. Dallas Rocks constantly changes its walls, giving climbers new routes and challenges every time. In the gym portion, the facility has a full-scale fitness center with cardio machines, free weights, heavy bags, and medicine balls, supervised by on-site trainers, coaches, nutritionists, and other health and athletic professionals.

Dallas Zoo (214-670-5656; www.dallaszoo.com) 650 South R. L. Thornton Freeway, Dallas 75203. Open: 9 AM–5 PM daily, except Christmas. Admission: Adults (13+) $12, children (3–12) and seniors (65+) $9; toddlers (0–2) free. Carousel is $2 and the monorail is $3 per rider. The Dallas Zoo is the largest zoological park in Texas. The park is sectioned into four areas: the entry plaza, where you will find information, stroller and wheelchair rentals, and lockers and feed tokens; a children's zoo where kids can get face-to-face with rabbits, miniature donkeys, and dwarf mongooses; Zoo North, which hosts the standard zoo animals such as giraffes, elephants, and kangaroos; and the Wilds of Africa, where you'll find the crocodile lake and the chimpanzee forest. A monorail runs throughout the park from 9:30 to 3:30 daily. Parking is $7 per vehicle.

Gondola Adventures, Inc. (1-866-646-2064; www.gondola.com/Home.asp) 357 West Fork, Irving 75039. Take a peaceful, private cruise along the Mandalay Canal and Lake Carolyn in a gondola. Gaze upon waterfall views with romantic music or singing, provided by the gondolier. Gondolas are either an electric or rowing vessel, and riders have their choice of several cruise types and can select anything from a simple cruise for two to a romantic dinner cruise to a full wedding, party, or corporate function. Gondola Adventures can also create a secret message-in-a-bottle experience for your journey. Your message is written on fine parchment, rolled tightly, tied with ribbon, and corked in a clear glass wine bottle. It is "found" while cruising and opened, revealing the surprise inside to its intended. The dinner cruises are catered and are ideal for wedding proposals, romantic evenings, or for someone looking for a unique experience.

Grapevine Opry (817-481-8733; www.grapevinetexasusa.com/Grapevine Opry/index.htm) 701 South Main Street, Grapevine 76051. Admission: Adults $15, children (0–12) $10.00. Come to the Grapevine Opry for some boot-scootin' boogie that will leave your hands clapping and your feet stomping. The Opry has grown to become one of the nation's best places to showcase tomorrow's music leg-

Insider tip: In addition to hosting performers from around the country, the Opry has a regular schedule of in-house events, including the Country Music Showcase, which is presented every Sat. evening at 7:30 PM, and the Gospel Country show is scheduled for the fourth Fri. of each month, beginning at 7:30 PM. Consult the website for the full roster of performances.

The Mandalay Canal in Irving. Irving CVB

ends today. The amphitheater also has a wonderful sound system and interior acoustics for top-notch listening enjoyment. While country music is the Opry's mainstay, the theater also proudly hosts a variety of genres, from 1950s rock and roll to gospel, bluegrass to big band, and even holiday tunes from visiting artists and its own highly acclaimed house band. Music and dancing provide fun for everyone in the family.

LEGOLAND Discovery Centre (www.legolanddiscoverycenter.com) 3000 Grapevine Mills Parkway, Grapevine 76051. One of only five in the world, this 35,000-square-foot indoor attraction located inside Grapevine Mills Mall offers children and their families an interactive and educational experience. Spend hours exploring and building inside the world's biggest box of Legos!

Lone Star Park (972-237-5000; www.lonestarpark.com) 1000 Lone Star Parkway, Grand Prairie 75050. Open: Fri. and Sat. gates open at 5:30 PM, first live race at 6:35 PM Admission: General (adults $5, children 4–12 $3, toddlers 0–3 free), clubhouse $8, apron seats $8, counter seats $9, ballroom or box seats $12 and up. At Lone Star Park, guests can enjoy the swiftness of the quarter horse, thoroughbreds, and other horse breeds as they gallop down the track. Wager on a race or two in this picturesque, world-

Insider tip: Visitors who purchase general admission tickets are welcome to bring blankets and lawn chairs for use in the grassy areas in both the picnic area and Post Time Pavilion, both of which have great views of the track.

Lone Star Park was home of the 2004 Breeders' Cup race.

Grapevine Vintage Railroad. Grapevine CVB

class racetrack. All guests are admitted to the first level, where concessions, wagering, and the gift shop are located, but it is standing room only. Upgraded tickets with assigned seats, however, are cheap and easy to obtain. The separate paddock area is a wonderful place to watch the jockeys and the trainers prepare for upcoming races, but it is also a nice place to watch the horses during race time. Guests can also upgrade to the clubhouse level to access both the second and fourth levels of the grandstand for climate-controlled views of the track. Persons under 18 must be accompanied by a parent, but bettors must be at least 21.

McDonald's (972-233-5952; www.mctexas.com/1755) 13105 Montfort Drive, Dallas 75240. The McDonald's at Montfort Drive is a bit different; it was built as the World's Biggest Happy Meal, or at least, an old-school version of one. Featured on The Travel Channel, this location has unusual external architecture and upscale interior decor. Inside it has Austrian crystal chandeliers, Ralph Lauren wallpaper, granite floors, mahogany booths, incandescent lighting, private lamps at each table, floral arrangements, and a modern ambiance that mitigates its fast-food feel. Even the restrooms are exquisite, with black marble countertops. On the exterior, visitors will find a large, fiberglass Big Mac above the door, as well as large statues of Ronald McDonald and his compatriots. Even the drive-through is lit like the night sky, dark with spare, twinkling lights above.

Medieval Times (1-866-543-9637; www.medievaltimes.com/dallas) 2021 North Stemmons Freeway, Dallas 75207. Open: Show times vary, primarily Thurs. through Sun. Admission: Adults $58.95, children $35.95. Step into the castle and out of this century. As a royal guest of King Philippe, you are transported to the 11th century and treated to dinner and an authentic medieval tournament (with the help of Hollywood-caliber special effects,

Insider tip: Check the Medieval Times website in advance for special pricing, as significant discounts and promotions are usually offered online, as well as package upgrades (sometimes for free) that include specialty seating, a commemorative program, and a behind-the-scenes DVD.

of course). There is also a bar, dance floor, Hall of Arms displaying medieval artifacts, and a medieval torture museum. Dress casually and be prepared to eat with your hands, as forks and spoons were not used in the 11th century.

Ripley's Believe it Or Not!, Louis Tussaud's Palace of Wax, and Ripley's Enchanted Mirror Maze (972-263-2391; grandprairie.ripleys.com) 601 East Palace Parkway, Grand Prairie 75050. Open: Various, depending on season. Admission: Various, depending on attraction. Located in one entertainment complex, there are three attractions. Ripley's Believe It or Not!, the main attraction, is home to 11 galleries covering more than 10,000 square feet of exhibits, interactive displays, illusions, and thousands of astonishing and unusual artifacts collected from the far corners of the world—all real and mind boggling. Meet 200+ lifelike movie stars and historical figures at Louis Tussaud's Palace of Wax in amazing detail. Finally, Ripley's Enchanted Mirror Maze has more than 100 mirrors with LED lighting and digital sound. With more than 2,000 square feet of back-to-back mirrors, it's up to you to find your way out of the labyrinth, with a different experience every time. Go through as many times as you like with your ticket. Tickets are available at one-, two-, or three-attraction rates.

Speed Zone (972- 247-7223; speedzone.com/site/Dallas) 11130 Malibu Drive, Dallas 75229. Open: Mon. through Thurs. 12 PM–10 PM, Fri. 12 PM–12 AM, Sat. 10 AM–12 AM, Sun. 11 AM–10 PM. Admission: $79.95 for four hours of unlimited driving. Put the pedal to the metal on one of their four go-kart tracks. Motor around the track at wild top speeds (at least for a go-kart) on Thunder Road, Top Eliminator Dragster, Slick Track, or Turbo Track. Speed Zone also features The Fireball, a "super loop"

Insider tip: Check the website for specials, coupons, and discounted days and times. Prices can be as much as 75 percent off.

rollercoaster that towers six stories high and is guaranteed to get knees knocking. The less daring can choose from mini-golf, an arcade, and a restaurant with a full bar.

Texas Theatre (214-941-0040; www.thetexastheatre.com) 231 West Jefferson Boulevard, Dallas 75208. Open: See schedule of events. Admission: Varies. A performing arts theater, the Texas Theatre is located in the Oak Cliff neighborhood of Dallas. Once a movie theater, it is more widely known as the place where Lee Harvey Oswald, President Kennedy's alleged assassin, was arrested. Oswald entered the Texas Theatre without paying for a ticket, ostensibly to avoid police, on November 22, 1963. The police were notified of the patron who did not pay, and the police apprehended the hiding Oswald. Today, the Texas Theatre is a community-run theater, playing indie and classic movies and housing special per-

In another bit of interesting history, the Texas Theatre, which opened in 1931, was the largest suburban movie theater in Dallas and part of a chain of theaters once owned by millionaire Howard Hughes.

formances. The theater is owned by the Oak Cliff Foundation, a nonprofit organization that is working to fully restore the infamous landmark. To commemorate Oswald's capture, the fifth seat from the aisle in the third-to-last row bears these words in gold paint, "Lee Harvey Oswald, November 22, 1963," noting the exact seat he occupied while hiding. The theater's website is unimpressive and difficult to navigate, but a visit to the theater, perhaps for their nightly 7:30 PM movie showing, is well worth the hassle for participating in a small slice of American history.

The Mustangs of Las Colinas Museum (214-223-7840; www.mustangsoflascolinas.com) 5205 North O'Connor Drive, Suite 155, Irving 75039. Open: 24 hours. Admission: Free. Located in the open air of Williams Square Plaza, The Mustangs of Las Colinas Museum is home to Ben H. Carpenter's vision. He hired an artist to create a sculpture that would capture the free spirit and the heritage of Texas. The resulting work of art, Irving's artistic centerpiece depicts a herd of wild mustangs like ones found in Texas's early days, galloping with determination across a prairie stream. Sculpted in bronze, the nine mustangs are startlingly realistic and powerful to see in person. The statues are about 1½ times life size, and the small fountains underneath give a visual of the horses splashing through the water. Nearby is an accompanying museum with a pictorial history and short film of how Robert Glen, the sculptor, created his installation. Visitors can purchase mustang souvenirs at the gift shop.

The Mustangs of Las Colinas. Irving CVB

Vetro Glass Blowing Studio and Art Studio (817-251-1668; www.vetroartglass.com) 701 South Main Street, Suite 103, Grapevine 76051. Open: Studio hours Sept. through June, Wed. through Sat. 10 AM–1 PM; closed July and Aug. for annual machine maintenance; Gallery hours Tues. through Sat. 10 AM–6 PM, Sun. 12 PM–5 PM. Admission: Free. Events: tours $2 (15-person minimum), workshop costs vary. Glass blobs are transformed into beautifully crafted translucent bowls, vases, sculptures, vessels, wine decanters, contemporary lighting installations, corporate awards, jewelry, decorative art pieces, and more. At Vetro, owner and artist David Gappa and his staff have an incredible collection of glass pieces on display and for sale. Visitors are invited to watch and learn about this ancient art form as they demonstrate the glassblowing processes of blowing, fusing, casting, and sculpting. Studio guests can get in on the artistry for themselves with Vetro's ongoing schedule of classes and workshops. Children are welcome to watch the demonstrations, but their behavior must be closely monitored by parents at all times for their own safety. Admission is free to the general public, but tips for the artists are appreciated.

Zero Gravity Thrill Amusement Park (972-484-8359; www.gojump.com) 11131 Malibu Drive, Dallas 75229. Open: Sun. through Thurs. 12 PM–11 PM, Fri. and Sat. 12 PM–1 AM. Admission: Ranges between $29 and $69, depending on ride selections. An "extreme rides amusement park" (with a 70 mph ride and a 16-story free fall), Zero Gravity treats guests to an unforgettable experience on one or all five of the adrenaline-pumping rides: Bungee Jump, Skyscraper, Nothin' But Net, Skycoaster, and/or Texas Blastoff. One-ride rates and five-ride packages are available.

Denton

Texas Woman's University First Ladies Collection (940-898-3644; www.twu.edu/gown-collection) 304 Administration Drive, Denton 76204. Open: Mon. through Fri. 8 AM–5 PM. Admission: Free. Much more than a sampling of pretty dresses, the First Ladies Collection is a chronicling of the gorgeous fashions owned by the wives of Texas governors. From the 1800s to today, each gown reflects the fabric, sewing styles, fashion trends, and sewing technologies of its time. These gowns also serve as a window into the minds, styles, and legacies of each woman who wore them as they contributed to the making of the state, each in their own way. There are more than 40 gowns in the collection, with about 20 on display at any given time. The dresses belonged to notable women like Laura Bush; Lady Bird Johnson; Mamie Eisenhower; Nellie Connally, known for her famous ride in the motorcade when President Kennedy was shot in 1963; and Marietta Garner, wife of Vice President John Garner under President Franklin Delano Roosevelt. The collection is located at the university's Hubbard Hall, near the intersection of Administration Drive and Bell Avenue. Weekend tours are available by appointment only.

Fort Worth

Billy Bob's Texas (817-624-7117; www.billybobstexas.com) 2520 Rodeo Plaza, Fort Worth 76164. Open: Mon. through Sat. 11 AM–2 AM, Sun. 12 PM–2 AM. Admission: Fri. and Sat. $1 before 5 PM, closed 5 PM–6 PM, Fri. and Sat. after 6 PM $10 and up, depending on the

Vetro Glass Blowing Studio. Grapevine CVB

Billy Bob's Texas has been the backdrop for many television shows and full-length movies. Episodes from the series *Dallas*, *Walker: Texas Ranger*, CBS's *Happy New Year America*, CBS *This Morning*, and the Nashville Network's *On Stage* have been shot on-site, as well as *Over the Top*, *Baja Oklahoma*, *Necessary Roughness*, and *Pure Country*. Billy Bob's Texas has also been in countless music videos from a variety of artists.

entertainment performance. Sun. through Tues. $1 before 7 PM or $3 after 7 PM, Wed. through Thurs. $1 before 8 PM or $4 after 8 PM. Live Bull Riding: Fri. and Sat. 9 PM and 10 PM, $2.50. Concerts and bull riding go hand in hand at Billy Bob's. Really, no bull . . . okay, well, a little bull. Every weekend, Billy Bob's hosts live country music performers from around the world. Up-and-coming stars, as well as country legends, have performed there, like Larry Gatlin and the Gatlin Brothers, Loretta Lynn, Waylon Jennings, Hank Williams Jr., Clint Black, Merle Haggard, Garth Brooks, and Willie Nelson. Tickets go on sale on the first of the month prior to the show and can be purchased online, in person, over the phone, or through Ticketmaster. They also serve barbeque, snacks, and fountain drinks in their restaurant. At its indoor arena, you can watch professional riders take on some of the toughest bulls anywhere; this is a spectator sport only. Billy Bob's is a family entertainment center, but know that alcohol is also served and an occasional adult-only event is scheduled. Parking from Sun. through Thurs. is free, unless there is a special event. Parking Fri. and Sat. is $5, and valet parking is $10 per car after 5 PM.

Bureau of Engraving and Printing (817-231-4000; www.moneyfactory.gov/tours/fort worthtxtours.html) 9000 Blue Mound Road. Fort Worth 76131. Open: Aug. through May, Mon. through Fri. 8:30 AM–3:30 PM; June and July, Mon. through Fri. 8:30 AM– 5:30 PM. Admission: Free. Tours: Every 30 minutes. The buck starts here! Learn about paper currency and how it is made. You will see a short film that introduces you to the facility and reveals part of the money-making process. Afterward, a tour guide will lead you through a series of enclosed, elevated walkways with windows, allowing you to peek over their production line at the various stages of the process. While you're there, you'll see billions of dollars being printed. It's awe inspiring, but don't get any funny ideas—

Insider tip: Go through the tour before examining the exhibits on the second floor—it will help you understand exactly what is that you will be seeing. The exhibits showcase the history of currency and the intricacies and mistakes of the printing process. Also, visit the restrooms first. It's hard to take a break once the tour has started. You will have to backtrack with an escort to get to a bathroom.

security is extremely tight. The tours are approximately 45 minutes long, and there is a gift shop filled with money-related items.

Fort Worth Herd (817-336-4373; www.fortworth.com/the-herd) 131 East Exchange Avenue, Suite 215, Fort Worth 76164. Open: daily, except Easter, Thanksgiving, or Christmas. Admission: Free. Event: 11:30 AM and 4 PM. Cattlemen drove their herds into Fort Worth and onward along the Chisholm Trail to the railroads for shipping eastward.

Fort Worth Herd at Stockyards Station. Fort Worth CVB

Those days are over, but the cattle-drive spirit lives on. Twice daily, longhorn steers are driven down historic Exchange Avenue in the Stockyards by real cowboys and cowgirls. The trail bosses, it should be noted, have the option of canceling a drive due to inclement weather or the changing temperaments of the cattle.

Insider tip: Get a table at any of the Stockyards Station restaurants with outdoor seating that faces East Exchange Avenue. Another good watch spot is the front lawn of the Livestock Exchange Building. Both areas are close, but not too close.

Insider Tip: The cowboys and cowgirls will happily talk about the tools, equipment, and techniques of the late 1800s cattle drive at the termination of the path at CowCamp. CowCamp is every Saturday and Sunday at 1:30 behind the Livestock Exchange Building at the corrals where the animals are kept from Memorial Day to Labor Day.

Fort Worth Nature Center and Refuge (817-237-1111; www.fwnaturecenter.org) 9601 Fossil Ridge Road, Fort Worth 76135. Open: Oct. through Apr., Mon. through Sun. 8 AM–5 PM; May through Sept., Mon. through Fri. 8 AM–7 PM, Sat. and Sun. 7 AM–7 PM. Admission: Adults $4, seniors (65+) $3, children (3–17) $2, children (0–2) free. See the wilderness as the early pioneers did. The Fort Worth Nature Center and Refuge, a still-hidden gem even for locals, is a 3,600-acre expanse of forests, prairies, and wetlands just 10 miles from downtown Fort Worth. Complete with native plants and wildlife, the center provides a myriad of natural wonders and a welcome respite for those looking for a slice of nature within an increasingly urban lifestyle. A prairie dog town and a bison range, as well as wild turkeys, armadillos, alligators, raccoons, skunks, bobcats, deer, squirrels, opossum, beaver, turtles, lizards, snakes, and more than 200 species of birds and 300 species of flowering plants, may be seen here.

Fort Woof Dog Park (817-871-5700; www.fortwoof.org) 750 North Beach Street, Fort Worth 76111. Open: Daily, 5 AM–11:30 PM. Admission: Free. Fort Worth's largest dog park, Fort Woof, located in Gateway Park, is the ideal place to take a traveling dog for some off-the-leash exercise and socialization. The park comprises two large fenced areas: one for larger dogs at 40 pounds and more; the other for smaller dogs. Each area has picnic tables (food is prohibited), park benches for humans, watering stations, and waste disposal stations. To be admitted, dogs must be licensed and current on their rabies vaccinations and tags. Puppies younger than four months old are prohibited, and owners are responsible for removal and disposal of droppings from their pets. Dogs in heat are also not allowed. The park is lighted for nighttime play.

The Fort Worth Water Gardens. Laura Heymann

Fort Worth Water Gardens (817-392-7111; www.fortworth.com/listings/index.cfm ?action=display&listingID=2989) 1502 Commerce Street, Fort Worth 76102. Open: 24 hours. Admission: Free. This is a concrete water garden—unconventional in materials and in beauty. Glistening in the sun during the day and sparkling under romantic lighting at night, the water gar-

> The 1976 movie *Logan's Run*, starring Michael York and Peter Ustinov, was shot partially at the Fort Worth Water Gardens.

den is an architectural and engineering wonder that is an elegant and refreshing oasis in busy downtown Fort Worth. The large main pool has water cascading down its 38-foot walls and terraces into a collection pool at the bottom, along with steps that guide visitors to the pool. Know that there are no handrails, and the slightest misstep can cause someone to fall into the drink. There are another three, unconnected meditation pools that are also wonderful to visit and are usually less crowded than the big pool.

The Fort Worth Zoo. Cesar Tapia

Fort Worth Zoo (817-759-7555; www.fort worthzoo.org) 1989 Colonial Parkway, Fort Worth 76110. Open: Hours vary by season. Admission: Adults (13+) $12, children (3–12) and seniors (65+) $9, toddlers (0–2) free. The Fort Worth Zoo has 12 permanent exhibit areas—Penguins,

> **Insider tip:** Enjoy half-price admission at the Fort Worth Zoo every Wednesday.

World of Primates, Asian Falls, Raptor Canyons, Cheetahs, Flamingo Bay, Meerkat Mounds, Australian Outback, African Savannah, Parrot Paradise, Texas Wild!, and the **Museum of Living Art (MOLA)**. Check their website ahead of time to find out about their ever-changing roster of rotating exhibits. Parking is $5 per vehicle, cash only. Stroller and motorized cart rentals are available; a limited number of wheelchairs are also available for use.

Marshall Creek Ranch (817-490-8796; www.marshallcreekranch.com) 4401 T.W. King Road, Southlake 76092. Sometimes, a person needs to get away from the city and enjoy a little bit of the rural life. Marshall Creek Ranch, located in Southlake north of Fort Worth, is a great place to get out into the wide open spaces and ride a horse. From beginner to advanced, the ranch is able to accommodate all levels of knowledge and experience of riding. Guides will take you and your horse along 2,200 acres of breathtaking trails on the shores of Lake Grapevine and unspoiled lands to enjoy the sounds of quiet. Marshall Creek Ranch also provides stabling for visitors with horses who are seeking a full level of care.

The Fort Worth Zoo. Cesar Tapia

The Fort Worth Zoo. Fort Worth CVB

Mrs. Baird's Bakery Tour (817-615-3050; www.mrsbairds.com/bakery/tour.php) 7301 South Freeway, Fort Worth 76134. Open: Tues. through Thurs. Admission: Free. There's nothing like the smell of warm baked goods. The bakery tour of Mrs. Baird's Bakery, a subsidiary of Bimbo Bakeries USA, encourages all noses to deeply breathe in their aromas. The bakery tour includes a visit of the facility that makes not only Mrs. Baird's bread but also Orowheat, Bimbo, Tia Rosa, Entenmann's, Thomas', and Marinela brand goods. The tour is educational for kids of all ages.

Insider tips: There are a few rules to adhere to in the bakery. You must make a reservation two weeks in advance, which can be made over the phone or through their website. Children must be at least six years old to participate, and one adult must be present for every 10 children. All legs must be covered with long pants, open-toed shoes are forbidden, sneakers with wheels are not allowed, and video cameras are not permitted.

The Fort Worth Zoo. Fort Worth CVB

NRH$_2$O Water Park (817-427-6500; www.nrh2o.com) 9001 Boulevard 26, North Richland Hills 76180. Open: Varies, depending on season. Admission: Adults and children 48 inches and over $23.99, children under 48 inches $19.99, children (0–2) free. Beat the Texas heat at NRH$_2$O Water Park. There are a variety of water rides and pools here for those looking for relaxation or adventure. The Green Extreme, a seven-story waterslide that propels riders upward with an incredible 1,161 feet of twists and turns, is their signature high-thrill ride. The Black Falls, Accelerator, Blue Twister, and Purplepalooza rides are equally exhilarating. The NRH$_2$ Ocean is a wave pool that also hosts family-friendly movies for free every Friday night. In the Tadpole Swimming Hole, little ones can slide down pint-size chutes. Catering is available, but coolers are also welcome. NRH$_2$O also offers free parking and free use of life jackets.

Plano

Southfork Ranch (972-442-7800; www.southfork.com) 3700 Hogge Road, Parker 75002. *Dallas*, the dramatic nighttime series that ran for 13 years on CBS, was filmed at Southfork Ranch in Parker, Texas, about 6 miles northeast of Plano. Visit the ranch to see the gun that famously shot J.R. and inspect Lucy's wedding dress. Take a tour around and through the famed Ewing mansion. The tour makes stops to see the Texas Longhorns and American quarter horses on the ranch's grounds, as well as Jock Ewing's original 1978 Lincoln Continental. Eat at Miss Ellie's Deli or take the chuck wagon dinner tour. Cowboys from the chuck wagon will entertain you with campfire songs and recite cowboy poetry over dinner. A minimum of 20 people are required for the dinner, but it can be expanded to accommodate as many as several hundred visitors. Leashed dogs are allowed on the grounds, but they are not allowed in buildings unless they can be carried. Southfork also hosts special events and has a hotel on-site.

DAY TRIPS

Dinosaur Valley State Park (254-897-4588; www.tpwd.state.tx.us/spdest/findadest/parks/dinosaur_valley) Glen Rose 76043. Open: Daily, 8 AM–10 PM. Admission: $5. Dinosaur Valley State Park contains some of the best-preserved dinosaur tracks in the world, at an estimated 113 million years old. These tracks reveal the subtle footsteps where area dinosaurs once traveled. At the entry of the park are two enormous dinosaur models, crafted by the New York World's Fair Dinosaur Exhibit in 1964–1965 and Sinclair Oil Company, whose mascot looks like one of the dinosaurs on display. The first is a 70-foot green Apatosaurus, and the other is a 45-foot Tyrannosaurus Rex. There are also places within the park to observe wildlife, camp, picnic, mountain bike, fish, swim, and walk along nature trails.

Dr Pepper Bottling Plant/Old Doc's Soda Shop (1-888-398-1024; www.olddocs.com) 105 East Elm, Dublin 76446. Open: Daily, 10 AM–5 PM. Admission: Adults $2.50, seniors (55+) $2, children (6–12) $2, children (0–6) free. Come see and taste Dr Pepper the way it was intended, made with pure cane sugar and bottled on a small scale. The original formula, which locals call Dublin Dr Pepper, can only be found in the immediate area and has a delicious flavor that most soda drinkers around the world do not know about. Most Dr

Pepper plants in decades past switched to high fructose corn syrup and fancy bottling machinery to save money, but not Dublin. Take the tour and then stop by the soda shop for sodas, floats, and other goodies made with the original Dr Pepper.

Insider tip: The Dr. Pepper plant does not bottle every day, but tours are offered every 45 minutes, regardless.

Eisenhower Birthplace (903-465-8908; www.visiteisenhowerbirthplace.com) 609 South Lamar Avenue, Denison 75021. Open: Tues. through Sat. 9 AM–5 PM, Sun. 1 PM–5 PM. Admission: Adults $4, children (6–18) $3, children (0–5) free. Visit the home in Denison, Texas, where the 34th U.S. President Dwight David "Ike"

An enterprising young man, Eisenhower sold corn and cucumbers to earn money. He also learned to make tamales from his mother's recipe, selling them at three for a nickel.

Eisenhower was born and lived. Filled with antique furniture from 1890, his year of birth, this modestly framed, two-story home reveals the life of the regular working-class family from which the future president and war hero emerged. The exhibit includes the home, the gardens, a portion of abandoned railroad track, and a larger-than-life statue of Eisenhower, as well as Ike memorabilia. The tour is guided. The Eisenhower Birthplace is located approximately 75 miles north of Dallas.

Fossil Rim Wildlife Center (254-897-2960; www.fossilrim.org) 2155 County Road 2008, Glen Rose, TX. Open: Varies, depending on season. Admission: Adults $20.95, seniors (65+) and children (3–11) $13.95, toddlers (0–2) free. Fossil Rim is home to about 1,000 individual animals belonging to 50 different species that roam freely around its 1,700 acres. To see them, you can opt for a scenic drive throughout or leave it to the experts on a guided tour. The center specializes in captive breeding programs for indigenous and exotic

A zipline tour is a fantastic way to take in the scenery. Courtesy of Wired

endangered species of animals. They also offer many educational programs and camps for children. Check their website ahead of time or call for their days/hours of operation and prices, as they are seasonal.

Wired (903-567-2681; www.ziptheusa .com) 796 North Trade Days Boulevard, Canton 75103. Open: Sat. and Sun. 9 AM–5 PM. Admission: $55. Wired is a zipline challenge course, a thrilling ride that travels over 20 acres of beautiful Texas terrain. A zipline is a long cable mounted on an incline that has a suspended pulley/harness system for riders. Each rider is accompanied by a trained and certified zipmaster. The four-line course hovers above a rolling meadow that cozies up to a creek. The lines range in length from 650 feet to the ultra-long 1000+ foot ride. The ziplines, themselves, are 1/2-inch ultrastrong aircraft cables and are inspected daily. The launch platforms and towers, safe and sturdy, are made of industrial-grade steel and are connected to one another by rope sky bridges. Before launching into the air, every rider is required to complete ground school, where you will learn everything you need to know to enjoy the course safely. Riders are taught the proper riding posture, speed control, braking, and self-rescue techniques. Located in Canton, Texas, Wired is less than an hour east of Dallas.

Insider tip: If you want an up-close-and-personal encounter, go on the feeding tour at the Center. Also, consult the website for significant discounts, such as midweek tours, early morning tours, and other special events.

Try a zipline tour . Courtesy of Wired

Insider tip: There are some physical requirements for riding along the Wired zipline; guests must be over the age of 10, wear closed-toe shoes, have long hair pulled back, and must sign a release (or have a parent/guardian present to sign a release). Bring current photo identification that reveals your age; reservations are recommended, but drop-ins are welcome.

The Perch Pond at Joe Pool Lake inside Cedar Hill State Park. Laura Heymann

PARKS AND RECREATION

There are a surprisingly large number of lakes and parks in the DFW area, and there is a good chance one will be near you. Fort Worth alone, for example, has 228 city parks. There are another 27 state parks and 66 lakes in North Texas. Rather than list them all, consider your area and what you would like to do there—hike, bike, swim, fish, boat, ski, and more—to help you select the right outdoor recreation spot. Below are just a few of the possible links available that will help you.

DFW is dotted with public golf courses far too numerous to mention here. To find a public course in Dallas, visit www.golfersweb.com /golfdfw/dallmap.htm. In Fort Worth, visit www.golfersweb.com/golfdfw/ftwmap.htm.

City Parks

www.arlingtontx.gov/park/index.html
www.dallasparks.org
www.cityofdenton.com/index.aspx?page=277
www.fortworthgov.org/pacs;
www.plano.gov/Departments/ParksAndRecreation/Pages/default.aspx
Lakes and State Parks www.tpwd.state.tx.us/spdest/findadest/prairies_and_lakes/dallas
    _and_fort_worth;
www.tpwd.state.tx.us/fishboat/fish/recreational/lakes/inplains.phtml

Golf is a very popular pastime in North Texas. Fort Worth CVBv

The sunset at Lake Arlington. Laura Heymann

8

Shopping

From Unique to Chic

Introduction

The shopping possibilities are endless in DFW, and there are at least 20 shopping malls within the region (listed in the second part of this chapter), but here, we will on focus on boutique-type shops, stores with interesting offerings, or ones that are conveniently near tourist attractions.

Dallas

Canton Trade Days 401 North Trade Days Boulevard Canton 75103. On the first Monday of each month, the city of Canton proudly hosts its Canton First Monday Trade Days, an outdoor flea market that lasts for several days and attracts visitors from all over Texas. Their website also has a listing of the exact dates. The outdoor vendors often begin setting up as early as the Monday prior in an area called "the hill" located west of Pavilion 4500. There is a map online that shoppers can print out in advance that can also give you a visual of the pavilion, as well as the entirety of the park. Not far away from Pavilion 4500 are the new pavilions, 6000 and 6500, atop the same hill. Begin shopping at the north end and work your way to the south end. A food court gives shoppers a place to rest and evaluate their purchases. If you adore shopping, rent a cart or bring a wagon to carry your bulky items, as goodies always seem to get heavier as the day progresses. Shoppers are invited to park in the market's designated RV parking area; both reserved and unreserved spaces are first-come-first-served.

> **Insider tip:** Dress for comfort; layers of clothing can always adjust to changing temperatures. Also, know that Texas has a large number of sunny days, and shoppers should bring sunscreen, water, and a hat, as many vendors are outdoors.

LEFT: *The Arlington Highlands, where dining and shopping abound.*

Dallas Design District (214-741-4748; www.dallas-design-district.com; www.design districtdallas.com) Located on the west side of I-35E at Oak Lawn Avenue, the Dallas Design District is a vibrant and expansive shopping area with an impressive collection of designer showrooms, antique shops and art galleries. Once a resource for designers only, this prestigious locale has now evolved into a specialized retail and wholesale area for home furnishings. Most of the retail shops and galleries are open Mon. through Sat. 10 AM–5 PM; visit the websites above for a directory of stores.

Insider tip: There are a handful of design centers that are still considered "for the design trade only," and do not allow browsing, but in general, most of the "on street" businesses are open to all customers.

Junkadoodle (214-350-5755; junkadoo-dle.com) 4402 West Lovers Lane, Dallas 75209. Open: Mon. through Sat. 10 AM–6 PM, Sun. 12 PM–5 PM. This place is heaven for those whose idea of shopping is not just the purchase but the love of the hunt. Junkadoodle is a boutique filled with funky, estate sale and whimsical, flea market–type merchandise from yesteryear and is brimming with interesting finds and novelty items. Rummage through their unique home accessories, fun furniture, and eccentric objects from the outlandish to the stylish. The management recommends circling through the shop three times on each visit, as there is so much to see that it cannot be comprehended in just one pass. The store has tons of original artwork, shabby chic furniture, various religious bric-a-brac, lighting, apparel, toys, and anything and everything imaginable. Step into the "backyard" of this converted home-

Treasures abound inside Junkadoodle. Monica Prochnow

A look inside the Make Shop & Studio. Monica Prochnow

turned-storefront, and you'll find an array of outdoor goods and signs, decor, and at last check, an antique travel trailer. Plan on spending at least an hour and a half there.

Lula B's (214-749-1929; www.lula-bs.com) 1010 Riverfront Boulevard, Dallas 75207. Open: Mon. through Sat. 10 AM–6 PM, Sun. 12 PM–6 PM. This isn't your grandmother's antique mall. "A treasure trove of all things fine and funky, kitschy and collectible, vintage and pimpadelic," Lula B's holds discoveries of every kind from several decades gone by. With 80 vendors and thousands of square feet, Lula B's provides a market for its shoppers to decorate and dress uniquely while sticking to a budget. Popular finds include vintage, eclectic, and mod fashions and jewelry; movie and music memorabilia; and vintage cowboy boots, cameras, collectible toys, and vinyl. There is a second location in the Deep Ellum neighborhood of Dallas.

Make Shop & Studio (214-256-3061; www.themakesite.com) 313 North Bishop Avenue, Dallas 75208. Open: Wed. through Sat. 12 PM–8 PM, and first Thursday of each month 12 PM–10 PM. In the heart of the Bishop Arts District in the Oak Cliff section of Dallas is Make, a women's apparel boutique that sells handcrafted goods made by local artisans. These are one-of-a-kind shirts, pants, skirts, dresses, scarves, purses, jewelry, hats, bags, and even some unique home decor pieces, but you will also pay for the level of craftsmanship. Make has only chic apparel that is beautiful and well made; they sell fashionable items that women want to wear. Think you can do better? Make also offers classes in sewing, screen printing, and crafting, teaching its students in a single afternoon how to make an article of clothing. Classes vary in price and length but tend to average around $50 and take about

Neiman Marcus goes all out with Christmas decorations at their downtown Dallas flagship store. Frank Goodenough

two hours to complete. The boutique also has open studio time for visitors to sew. The website has a calendar of ongoing classes.

Interesting tip: Two or three times per year, Make hosts the Urban Street Bazaar, a trunk show and handcrafted goods festival. Each bazaar has about 60 vendors, live performances, and plenty of food.

Neiman Marcus (214-741-6911; www .neimanmarcus.com) 1618 Main Street, Dallas 75201. Open: Mon. through Sat. 10 AM–6 PM, Thurs. 10 AM–7 PM, closed Sun. For a luxe shopping experience, home to the most exclusive designers (Gucci, Fendi, Prada, Valentino, Oscar de la Renta, Versace, La Perla, Roberto Cavalli, and Yves Saint Laurent), you know where to go.

Neiman Marcus was founded in Dallas, and it's the home of its flagship store.

Riddell Rare Maps & Fine Print (214-953-0601; www.antiquemapshop.com) 2611 Fairmount Street, Dallas 75201. Open: Tues. through Sat. 10 AM–6 PM.

Insider tip: If you're visiting Dallas during the holiday season, you simply must see Neiman's over-the-top window displays and amazing lighting.

History lovers and cartographers must get to this store as fast as they can. Prepare to be wowed by exquisite antique maps, engravings, lithographs, and other artwork from centuries past. The items, sometimes in color, depict places and persons from all over: Texas, the American West, the southwest, Canada, Mexico, the Western hemisphere, and even the globe. Bring your checkbook, because this type of authenticity in well-preserved and high-quality historical documents comes with a price tag, but there is nothing like owning a chart of the seas from the year 1596 or an 1825 map of Mexico with present-day United States acreage included. Unsurprisingly, this husband-and-wife-owned shop carries a lot of Republic of Texas ephemera.

Traders Village (972-647-2331; www.tradersvillage.com/en/grandprairie) 2602 Mayfield Road, Grand Prairie 75052. Open: Sat. and Sun. 8 AM—dusk. America's largest weekend flea market, Traders Village brings terrific values to thousands of visitors every year. Traders Village has everything from trash to treasure among its 3,500 dealers at bargain prices. Traders Village has a variety of food vendors, kids' rides, and games, as well as ATMs, stroller and wheelchair rentals, and modern restrooms on-site. Annual festivals like the National Championship American Indian Pow Wow and the Prairie Dog Chili Cook-off are also held there. Most of the vendors take credit cards or checks, but bring cash, because you never know what you will find. Also, pack a few dollars for parking, as well as suntan lotion, a bottle of water, a pair of good shoes for walking, and plenty of endurance to get through all the shops.

DENTON

Booked Up Inc. (940-574-2511; www.bookedupac.com) 216 South Center, Archer City 76351. Open: Mon. through Sat. 10 AM—5 PM. Booked Up, located about two hours northwest of Fort Worth, is a wonderful retailer of fine, rare, and scholarly books in its own right. However, the largest gem that awaits you in this store is not any particular item that can be found on any shelf; it is its Academy Award—winning screenwriter and Pulitzer Prize—winning author and shop owner, Larry McMurtry. He is most well known for his 1985 novel-turned-television series *Lonesome Dove*, a historical saga that follows ex—Texas Rangers as they drive their cattle from the Rio Grande, but also for his books-turned-movies *The Last Picture Show* and *Terms of Endearment*, and for cowriting the adapted screenplay *Brokeback Mountain*. In his shop, which does not sell any of his books, he sells more than 300,000 items arranged whimsically through four separate build-

Insider tip: If you want one of Larry McMurtry's titles, you'll have to go to Three Dog Books, a secondary store, located between Booked Up building #4 and the historic Royal Theater.

ings; sadly, a complete list of the inventory does not exist, and finding the gems within the stacks is an adventure unto itself. It's easy to spend hours here sorting through all of the books and oh-so-casually hanging out and waiting for McMurtry to appear. Local lore has it that he prefers to hang out in the first building near the big comfy chairs and air-conditioning. McMurtry is normally pegged as a recluse, but if he's in the store, he is known to be quite friendly.

Justin Discount Boots. Monica Prochnow

FORT WORTH

Justin Discount Boots (817-430-8084; www.justindiscountbootsonline.com) 101 Highway 156, Justin 76247. Open: Mon. through Sat. 9 AM–6 PM. When in Texas, do as the cowboys do. Deals on cowboy boots and other western apparel can be found at the Justin Boots company in its namesake town of Justin, Texas, about 28 miles north of Fort Worth but not as far north as Denton. Justin Boots doesn't have just one store but a few locations all within walking distance of one another, and they all carry discounted prices on Justin-brand boots, as well as those of its sister companies: Tony Lama Boots, Chippewa Boots, and Nocona Boots, all at below regular retail price. The shop has apparel for men, women, and children in all sizes and styles. Justin Boots has offered high-quality western apparel to the locals and across the world since 1897. Its customers have included Gene Autry, Ronald Reagan, Jack Benny, Gregory Peck, Dale Earnhardt, Randy White, Nolan Ryan, George Strait, and Dallas Cowboys owner Jerry Jones. The service is extremely polite. Justin is a small town that rests at the intersection of Farm Roads 407 and 156, a popular truck route, so be careful when walking across the road.

M.L. Leddy's Boots & Saddlery (1-888-565-2668; www.leddys.com) 2455 North Main Street, Fort Worth 76164. Visit M.L. Leddy's for custom made men's and women's western clothing, saddles, boots (traditional cowboy and vaquero), hats, buckles, stirrups, chaps, and tack to fit your body and your body alone. Located in both the Fort Worth Stockyards and Sundance Square downtown, their goods are handmade from start to finish. All of their products are made using the finest materials available, by experienced craftspeople. Leddy's speciality, however, is in boots, and if you purchase a pair of boots, the staff will measure your feet, cut the leather, custom stitch your boots, and stamp them with a customer number on the inside, meaning that your personal dimensions will forever be on their customer roster and completely accessible with that number. Never again will you ever need to be measured. You can order boots years from now thousands of miles away, and Leddy's will make a perfect pair for you as if you were there all along.

Peters Bros. Hat Company (817-335-1715; pbhats.com) 909 Houston Street, Fort Worth 76102. The Peters Bros. Hat Company is a custom hatmaker that sells cowboy hats, dress hats, straw hats, borsalino hats, Stetsons, and more in downtown Fort Worth. Our favorite was the Indiana Jones–style fedora for only $125. Pick a hat style, color, and fabric (felt or straw), and Peters Bros.'s in-store hatmaker will measure your head and create the perfect-fitting hat for you. They can even create the perfect hat, based on a photo or news clipping that you can bring in. Of course, the craftspeople there will not be able to make your hat on the spot; for them, it's a matter of craftsmanship, and your hat can be made within a few days or a few weeks, depending on your order and their waiting list. Peter Bros. also has repair services, which includes the cleaning and blocking of hats. If you don't have a hat of your own before leaving Fort Worth, your visit is incomplete.

PLANO

IKEA (972-712-4532; www.ikea.com/us/en/store/frisco) 7171 IKEA Drive, Frisco 75034. Open: Mon. through Sat. 10 AM–9 PM, Sun. 10 AM–7 PM. IKEA is an international company, but with so few locations in the United States, it was worth a mention in this book. IKEA is a warehouse store filled with affordable home goods that have a distinctive European flair. If it's for the home, and sometimes for the office, it can be found at IKEA. This store sells everything from bedroom furniture to crockery, cooking gadgets to gardening tools, shower curtains to laminate flooring, light fixtures to kitchen cabinetry, and major appliances to fabric. Upon entering the store, you are whisked upstairs by an escalator where countless mini living rooms, bedrooms, kitchens, and more are set up. It may feel invasive, as if you're intruding in someone's house, but walk through each room and examine the furnishings where each item is tagged with a price, color options, and aisle/bin numbers. Write these down, and find them later boxed up in the warehouse portion. Stop at the snack bar for cheap hot dogs or sodas, or stay for a meal in their in-house restaurant. The Swedish meatballs and the lingonberry jelly served with it are both knockouts. Bring an empty backseat or trunk, as it is impossible to leave there empty-handed. Newcomers should expect their first shopping trip to take three or four hours to review it all, and it is not unusual to feel overwhelmed. Assembly is required on many of their items, but tools and instructions are always included.

Sam Moon (214-297-4200; www.sammoon.com) 2449 Preston Road, Frisco 75034. Open: Mon. through Sat. 9:30 AM–7 PM. This place is the mecca of inexpensive costume jewelry and accessories. Come in for handbags, luggage, costume jewelry, sterling silver, cross necklaces, tiaras, costume jewelry, watch, hair accessories, rings, bracelets, anklets, broaches, wallets, belts, backpacks, hats, scarves, charms, handkerchiefs, lipstick cases, sunglasses, coin purses, hair extensions, and yes, even men's ties. Items come in all prices and styles from the wild and flashy to the dainty and classic, and no outfit will go without accessories after a visit to this place. Be aware that strollers are prohibited on Saturdays, as the store is packed with people, and it can create a hazard. Bring your patience because this place is always busy. If you have time, stop at its other neighboring shops selling home decor and luggage. Two additional locations—one in Dallas and one in Fort Worth.

Insider tip: Every August, Texas has a tax-free weekend in preparation for the back-to-school season. During a three-day, Friday through Sunday period, all apparel (boys, girls, men, and women), shoes, and school supplies are sold without tax. The date varies each year, but check the Texas Comptroller of Public Accounts website for exact information.

SHOPPING CENTERS AND MALLS

Arlington

Arlington Highlands (www.arlingtonhighlands.com) Stretching along the north side of I-20 between Collins Street and Matlock Road, Arlington, TX. Notables: Ann Taylor Loft, Brighton Collectibles, Coldwater Creek, Ethan Allen, Famous Footwear, James Avery, Justice for Girls, Sunglass Hut, Ulta, White House/Black Market, and World Market. Arlington Highlands is also dotted with restaurants and nightlife throughout.

The Arlington Highlands

Lincoln Square (817-461-7953; www
.lincolnsquarearlington.com) 436
Lincoln Square, Arlington 76011.
Notables: Ann Taylor Loft, Chico's, The
Children's Place, Claire's, Gap, Lane
Bryant, Rack Room Shoes, Ross, and
Talbots.

The Parks at Arlington (817-467-0200;
www.theparksatarlington.com) 3811
South Cooper Street, Arlington 76015.
Notables: Nordstrom Rack, Abercrombie
& Fitch, AMC 18 Theaters, M·A·C
Cosmetics, Build-A-Bear Workshop,
and a year-round ice-skating rink for
the kids.

Dallas
Firewheel Town Center (972-675-1041;
www.simon.com/mall/?id=1074) 245
Cedar Sage Dr., Suite 200, Garland 75040.
Notables: Ann Taylor Loft, Chico's, Dick's
Sporting Goods, DSW, Talbots, Victoria's
Secret, and Macy's.

Galleria Dallas (972-702-7100; www
.galleriadallas.com) 13350 Dallas Parkway,
Dallas 75240. Notables: Armani
Exchange, BCBG, bebe, Gucci, Godiva Chocolate, Michael Kors, Tiffany & Co., Tommy
Bahama, Juicy Couture, and a year-round ice-skating rink for the kids.

Grapevine Mills Malls (972-724-4910; www.simon.com/mall/default.aspx?id
=1248) 3000 Grapevine Mills Parkway, Grapevine 76051. Notables: Oakley Vault, Victoria's
Secret, New York and Company, Lane Bryant Outlet, Ecko Unlimited, Van's Outdoor, Sears
Outlet, Rack Room Shoes, Nike Factory
Outlet, Sanrio, Horchow by Neiman
Marcus, and Levi's Outlet.

Highland Park Village (214-528-9401;
www.hpvillage.com) 32 Highland Park
Village, Dallas 75205. Notables:
Anthropologie, Bang & Olufsen, Carolina
Herrera, Chanel Boutique, Christian
Louboutin, Cole Haan, Diane von
Furstenberg, Hermes, Harry Winston,
Jimmy Choo, Ralph Lauren, and
Williams-Sonoma.

Insider tip: Parking can be a problem on
weekend nights as the stores begin to close
and the entertainment comes to life. Arrive
around 10 AM for the best shopping or stake
your claim in the late afternoon if you plan to
stay and dine; otherwise, be prepared to surrender to the valet in Lincoln Square.

Insider tip: Lincoln Square offers bus service to the Ballpark and free Cowboys Stadium
event parking with an optional $10 shuttle for
its shopping and/or dining customers. For
game days and other major events, some
stores and restaurants open early as well.

During the holidays, visit Galleria Dallas. It is
home of the country's tallest Christmas tree.

Highland Park Village, built in 1931, was the
first planned shopping center in the United
States.

Northpark Center was the first air-conditioned
mall in the United States.

With the Westin Galleria as the anchor hotel to this popular upscale mall. Galleria Dallas provides a one-stop shopping experience. Dallas CVB/Courtesy of the Galleria, Dallas

Choices! Choices! Choices! From couture to casual, Galleria Dallas has it all.

Dallas CVB/Courtesy of the Galleria, Dallas

NorthPark Center (214-361-6345; www.northparkcenter.com) 8687 North Central Expressway, Dallas 75225. Notables: Barney's New York, Aveda, Burberry, Bulgari, Cartier, Coach, Cole Haan, Dooney & Bourke, Ed Hardy, Kate Spade, Louis Vuitton, Michael Kors, McCormick & Schmick's, Nine West, Oscar de la Renta, Ralph Lauren, Roberto Cavalli, Valentino, and Versace.

Richardson Square (972-675-1041; www.simon.com/Mall/?id=221) 501 South Plano Road, Richardson 75081. Notables: Super Target, Sears, Ross Dress for Less, Anna's Linens, and Lowe's.

Tanger Outlet Center (972-524-6034; www.tangeroutlet.com/terrell) 301 Tanger Drive, Terrell 75160. Notables: Bass, Haggar, Bon Worth, Gap Outlet, L'eggs Hanes Bali Playtex, Van Heusen, Levi's

Grapevine Mills Mall in Grapevine. Grapevine CVB

Outlet, Jockey, Reebok, Nike Factory Store, Le Gourmet Chef, and Wilson's Leather Outlet.

Town East Mall (972-270-2363; www.towneastmall.com) 2063 Town East Mall, Mesquite 75150. Notables: Charlotte Russe, New York & Co., Coach, Dickies and More, Express, G by Guess, Verizon Wireless, White Barn Candle Co., and Hot Topic.

Valley View Center (972-661-2939; www.shopvalleyviewcenter.com) 13331 Preston Road, Dallas 75240. Notables: JC Penney, Sears, Victoria's Secret, Naturalizer, American Eagle Outfitters, and Footlocker.

Denton
Golden Triangle Mall (940-566-6024; www.shopgoldentriangle.com) 2201 South I-35E, Denton 76205. Notables: Barnes and Noble, Sears, Spencer Gifts, Macy's, Hollister, Dillard's, and Aeropostale.

Vista Ridge Mall (972-315-3641; www.vistaridgemall.com) 2401 South Stemmons Freeway (I-35), Lewisville 75067. Notables: Macy's, Wet Seal, T-Mobile, Gap, Game Stop, Cinemark 15, and Sunglass Hut.

Fort Worth
Hulen Mall (817-294-1205; www.hulenmall.com) 4800 South Hulen Street, Fort Worth 76132. Notables: Brighton Collectibles, New York and Company, Charlotte Russe, Eddie

Bauer, Fossil, Frederick's of Hollywood, Hot Topic, Limited, and Journeys.

La Gran Plaza (817-922-8888; www.la granplazamall.com) 4200 South Freeway, Fort Worth 76115. Notables: Burlington Coat Factory, Foot Locker, Factory 2 U.

North East Mall (817-284-3427; www .simon.com/Mall/?id=220) 1101 Melbourne Road, Hurst 76053. Notables: Dillard's, Macy's, JCPenney, Nordstrom, Dick's Sporting Goods, Coach, Abercrombie & Fitch, Eddie Bauer, Godiva Chocolatier, Brighton Collectibles, Barnes & Noble, Old Navy, PetSmart, Dress Barn, and Ulta.

Ridgmar Mall (www.ridgmar.com) 1888 Green Oaks Road, Fort Worth 76116. Notables: Ann Taylor, Christopher and Banks, Dillard's, Macy's, Merle Norman, Origins, Rave Motion Pictures, Things Remembered, and Wet Seal.

Southlake Town Square (817-329-5566; www.southlaketownsquare.com) 1256 Main Street, Southlake 76092. Notables: Aeropostale, Anthropologie, bebe, Brooks Brothers, J. Crew, White House/Black Market, Lucky, Crate & Barrel, Oakley, and Pottery Barn.

Sundance Square (817-255-5700; www.sundancesquare.com) 201 Main Street, Fort Worth 76102. Notables: Jos. A. Banks, Retro Cowboy, Thomas Kinkade Gallery, Leddy's Ranch at Sundance, and Haltom's Jewelers.

> Along Camp Bowie Boulevard, starting in downtown Fort Worth and going south, you can explore more than 30 blocks of fabulous shopping, including some of the finest upscale specialty boutiques and lots of unique indie shops in the city—it's worth exploring.

Plano

Allen Premium Outlets (972-678-7000; www.premiumoutlets.com/outlets/outlet .asp?id=5) 820 West Stacy Road, Allen 75013. Notables: Aeropostale, BCBG, Chico's, Converse, Ecko Unltd., Eddie Bauer, Gap, Guess, J. Crew, Juicy Couture, Kenneth Cole, Le Creuset, Levi's, Nautica, Neiman Marcus Last Call, Official Dallas Cowboys Pro Shop, Perry Ellis, Puma, and True Religion.

Centre at Preston Ridge Mall (972-668-2986; www.centroprop.com/PropertyProfile _short.asp?ProjectID=PTXPREST1) 8400 Gaylord Parkway, Frisco 75034. Notables: Best Buy, DSW, Stein Mart, Tuesday Morning, Ulta Salon, and Big Lots.

Collin Creek Mall (972-422-1070; www.collincreekmall.com) 811 North Central Expressway, Plano 75075. Notables: Rave, Sears, Godiva Chocolate, Forever 21, Vans, Zumiez, and Journeys.

Stonebriar Centre (972-668-6255; www.shopstonebriar.com) 2601 Preston Road, Frisco 75034. Notables: Jessica McClintock, Ann Taylor Loft, Banana Republic, Aveda, Macy's, bebe, Nordstrom, Brighton Collectibles, Origins, Cache, Pottery Barn, Cheesecake Factory, Talbot's, Williams-Sonoma, Harry and David, and White House/Black Market.

The Shops at Willow Bend (972-202-7110; www.shopwillowbend.com) 6121 West Park Boulevard, Plano 75093. Notables: Aritizia, Anthropologie, Crate & Barrel, Lacoste, Brooks Brothers, Teavana, Sephora, Apple, and M·A·C Cosmetics.

9

INFORMATION

Know Before You Go

A trip to the Dallas–Fort Worth area, whether it is for business or pleasure, should be seamless and enjoyable. To help you prepare for your trip, we've included basic information that you may need while in the Metroplex.

AMBULANCE, FIRE, AND POLICE

Dial 911 for all ambulance, fire, and police services anywhere in the Metroplex. Cell phone towers will connect you to the nearest emergency service provider, regardless of your location or the origination of your phone number.

For nonemergency police services, dial 214-744-4444 for Dallas, 817-335-4222 for Fort Worth, 817-459-5200 for Arlington, 940-349-8181 for Denton, and 972-424-5678 for Plano.

EMERGENCY SERVICES

Contact emergency services in case of flood, tornados, or any other large-scale event.
Arlington Emergency Services, 817-543-5909
Dallas Office of Emergency Management, 214-670-4275

Denton Emergency Services, 940-349-2840
Fort Worth Emergency Management, 817-392-6170
Plano Emergency Operations Center, 972-769-4824
National Weather Service, Dallas–Fort Worth, 817-429-2631

AREA CODES

The Dallas–Fort Worth Metroplex is mainly served by the area codes 214, 972, 469, 682, and 817. Ten-digit dialing is standard, meaning you must dial the area code to call any number, even from a phone within the same area.

BIBLIOGRAPHY

Fiction

Living Dead in Dallas (Sookie Stackhouse/True Blood) by Charlaine Harris
Literary Dallas by Frances Brannen Vick (Guide to Dallas fiction with excerpts)
To Love and Die in Dallas by Mary Elizabeth Goldman
Fort Worth by Leonard Sanders
Literary Fort Worth by Judy Alter and James Ward Lee (Guide to Fort Worth fiction with excerpts)
Jitter Joint by Howard Swindle

History

Dallas Then and Now by Ken Fitzgerald
Historic Photos of Dallas by Michael V. Hazel
Dallas: A History of "Big D" by Michael V. Hazel
Historic Dallas Parks by John H. Slate and Dallas Municipal Archives
Historic Photos of Fort Worth by Quentin McGown
Gamblers & Gangsters: Fort Worth's Jacksboro Highway in the 1940s & 1950s by Ann Arnold
Fort Worth: A Texas Original! by Richard F. Selcer
Fort Worth and Tarrant County: An Historical Guide by Carol Roark
Fort Worth Then and Now by Carol E. Roark, Rodger Mallison, and Douglas Harman
Hell's Half Acre: The Life and Legend of a Red-Light District by Richard F. Selcer
They Came to Stay: The Story of the Jews of Dallas, 1870–1997 by Rose G. Biderman
Deep Ellum and Central Track: Where the Black and White Worlds of Dallas Converged by Alan B. Govenar and Jay F. Brakefield

Humor

Kinky Friedman's Guide to Texas Etiquette: Or How to Get to Heaven or Hell Without Going Through Dallas–Fort Worth by Kinky Friedman

Nonfiction

Boys Will Be Boys: The Glory Days and Party Nights of the Dallas Cowboys Dynasty by Jeff Pearlman
The Road to Dallas: The Assassination of John F. Kennedy by David E. Kaiser

At the State Fair Laura Heymann

60 Hikes Within 60 Miles: Dallas, Fort Worth: Includes Tarrant, Collin and Denton Counties by Joanie Sánchez

The Book Lovers Tour of Texas by Jesse Gunn Stephens

The Lives and Times of Dallas Black Women by Marc Sanders and Ruthe Winegarten

General Ike: A Personal Reminiscence by John S. D. Eisenhower

CHILD CARE

SeekingSitters (1-888-41-sitter (24-hour national line); Fort Worth, 817-900-8097; Dallas, 214-432-9002; Denton and Northeast Tarrant County, 817-789-1500; www.seek ingsitters.com) SeekingSitters is a babysitting referral service that offers full-time, part-time, onetime, and even last-minute babysitting requests. SeekingSitters does all of the work; they personally interview and screen each babysitting candidate. The sitters can come to you or meet you at your location. Rates vary.

Caring Hands (214-520-1191; www.caringhands.net) Caring Hands provides the finest registry of prescreened, qualified babysitters that come to you in your DFW-area homes, hotels, churches, and special events. Whether it's a wedding or a corporate trade show, children can enjoy high-quality care and fun, participating in planned activities and mini-camps.

Kids Park (817-236-1253; www.kidspark.com) 309 Curtis Mathes, Arlington 76018. Hourly childcare for children aged 2 to 12. The Kids Park facility is open days, evenings, and weekends without reservations or long-term commitments. The children are able to enjoy games, art, music, and just being with other kids.

CLIMATE AND WEATHER

January, February, and March:

The first three months of the year are the coldest in the Metroplex. The average temperature in January is 43 degrees, February is 47 degrees, and March is 56 degrees. About 14 days in each January, the weather drops below freezing, is cloudy about 16 days per month, and ranges between 62 percent and 80 percent humidity. February has about eight days per month that drop below freezing, has about 13 cloudy days, and ranges between 60 percent and 79 percent humidity. About three days in the month of March are below freezing, about 14 are cloudy, and ranges between 58 percent and 79 percent in humidity. It is during this time that many freeze warnings occur, and local bridges and roadways become iced over, creating hazardous driving conditions.

April, May, and June:

The second quarter of the year has the most pleasant weather in the Metroplex. The average temperature in April is 65 degrees, May is 72 degrees, and June is 81 degrees. The humidity in April ranges between 58 percent and 81 percent. May humidity ranges between 62 percent and 86 percent. June ranges between 58 percent and 85 percent in humidity. The weather is comfortable, and the sun is bright. There are about five days in May and 20 days in June that have temperatures over 90 degrees. The grasses are bright green, trees are revitalized from their winter sleep, and the bluebonnets and Indian paintbrush flowers are in full bloom, even if for only a brief time. This may explain, in part, the allergy misery that also accompanies the lovely landscape. These three months have the highest amount of pollen in the air and rain in the year.

July, August, and September:

These three months are the hottest in the Metroplex. The average temperature in July and August is 85 degrees, and September is 78 degrees. About 28 days in July have weather above 90 degrees, August has about 27 days, and September has about 15 days. Humidity in June ranges between 58 percent and 85 percent, July ranges between 52 percent and 80 percent, and August ranges between 52 percent and 79 percent. People should drink plenty of water and be mindful about the amount of time they spend outdoors.

October, November, and December

Over the final three months of the year, the temperature drops in large increments. The average temperature in October is 67 degrees, November dips to 56 degrees, and December is a crisp 47 degrees. About three days in November drop below freezing, and another 10 days in December. Humidity in October ranges between 57 percent and 82 percent, November ranges between 60 percent and 81 percent, and December ranges between 62 percent and 80 percent. The skies become muddled again, with 10 cloudy days in October, 12 in November, and 14 in December. It is not unusual to get a light snow, here or there, with flakes that do not stick. Most snows that stick usually occur after the new year, though roads can still ice over.

SPECIAL NEEDS SERVICES

Visitors with special needs should find DFW relatively easy to navigate. Most hotels, shops, restaurants, museums, and theaters have modern accommodations and access for people of all needs. Contact the front desk, ticket office, or customer service counter in advance for special requests or inquire about the availability of services. The Metroplex contains a mix of both old and new architecture, and challenges you may encounter, if any, are likely to come from smaller businesses in older storefronts or from old homes-turned-businesses. Dallas's public transportation system, DART (214-515-7272), and Fort Worth's T (817-215-8600) both offer assistance to the mobility-impaired offering door-to-door service with advance notice, and their jointly owned Trinity Railway Express (contact either DART or the T for info) is also able to accommodate riders with special needs. Visitors can also contact Avis & Scootaround Rental Program toll free (1-888-441-7575) or CVI Medical (1-866-340-7337) in either Dallas or Fort Worth to rent electric mobility scooters and wheelchairs for use while traveling.

HOSPITALS

Arlington

Kindred Hospital (817-960-3400) 1000 North Cooper, Arlington 76011.
Kindred Hospital Mansfield (817-473-6101) 1802 Highway 157 North, Mansfield 76063
Methodist Mansfield Medical Center (682-622-2000) 2700 East Broad Street, Mansfield 76063
Texas Health Arlington Memorial Hospital (817-548-6100) 800 West Randol Mill Road, Arlington 76012.
USMD Hospital at Arlington (817-472-3400) 801 Interstate 20, W. Arlington 76017.

Dallas

Baylor University Medical Center at Dallas (214-820-0111) 3500 Gaston Avenue, Dallas 75246.
Baylor Medical Center at Carrollton (972-492-1010) 4343 North Josey Lane Carrollton 75010.
Baylor Medical Center at Frisco (214-407-5000) 5601 Warren Parkway, Frisco 75034.
Baylor Medical Center at Garland (972-487-5000) 2300 Marie Curie Boulevard Garland 75042.
Baylor Medical Center at Irving (972-579-8100) 1901 North MacArthur Boulevard Irving 75061.
Charlton Methodist Hospital (214-947-7777) 3500 West Wheatland Road, Dallas 75237.
Children's Medical Center (214-640-2000) 1935 Medical District Drive, Dallas 75235
Doctor's Hospital of Dallas (214-324-6100) 9440 Poppy Drive, Dallas 75218.
Kindred Hospital (214-355-2600) 9525 Greenville Avenue, Dallas 75243.
Medical City Hospital (972-566-7000) 7777 Forest Lane, Dallas 75230.
Methodist Hospital of Dallas (214-947-8181) 1441 North Beckley Avenue, Dallas 75203.
Parkland Health (214-266-0100) 5201 Harry Hines Boulevard, Dallas 75235.
Presbyterian Hospital Dallas (214-345-6789) 8200 Walnut Hill Lane, Dallas 75231.

Fort Worth

Baylor All Saints Medical Center at Fort Worth (817-926-2544) 1400 Eighth Avenue, Fort Worth 76104.

Baylor Regional Medical Center at Grapevine (817-481-1588) 1650 West College Street, Grapevine 76051.

Cook Childrens Medical Center (682-885-4000) 801 Seventh Avenue, Fort Worth 76104

Harris Methodist Hospital Fort Worth (917-685-2000) 1301 Pennsylvania Avenue, Fort Worth 76104.

Harris Methodist HEB (817-685-4000) 1600 Hospital Parkway Bedford 76022.

Harris Methodist Southwest Hospital (817-433-5000) 6100 Harris Parkway, Fort Worth 76132.

John Peter Smith Hospital (817-921-3431) 1500 South Main, Fort Worth 76104.

Kindred Hospital (817-332-4812) 815 Eighth Avenue, Fort Worth 76104.

Texas Health Burleson (817-782-8000) 2750 S.W. Wilshire Boulevard Burleson 76028.

Denton

Denton Community Hospital (940-898-7000) 207 North Bonnie Brae, Denton 76201.

Denton Regional Medical Center (940-384-3535) 3535 South Interstate 35, Denton 76210.

Harris Methodist Northwest Hospital (817-444-8600) 108 Denver Trail Azle 76020.

Presbyterian Hospital Denton (940-898-7000) 207 North Bonnie Brae Street, Denton 76201.

Plano

Baylor Regional Medical Center at Plano (469-814-2000) 4700 Alliance Boulevard, Plano 75093.

Children's Medical Center at Legacy (469-303-7000) 7601 Preston Road, Plano 75024

Presbyterian Hospital Plano (972-981-8000) 6200 West Parker Road, Plano 75093.

Local Media

PRIMARY NEWSPAPERS

Dallas Morning News
Fort Worth Star-Telegram

SPECIALTY NEWSPAPERS

Dallas Voice, GLBT
La Estrella, Spanish language
Dallas Business Journal
Fort Worth Business Press
Fort Worth Weekly, city/entertainment guide
Dallas Observer, city/entertainment guide
Quick, city/entertainment guide
FD Luxe, style & fashion

MAGAZINES
Brides of North Texas
D Magazine, D CEO, D Home, D Weddings
Fort Worth
Fort Worth Child/Dallas Child
Texas Monthly

TELEVISION
KDTN, Channel 2 (Daystar)
KNPK, Channel 3 (Independent)
KDFW, Channel 4 (Fox)
KXAS, Channel 5 (NBC)
WFAA, Channel 8 (ABC)
KTVT, Channel 11 (CBS)
KERA, Channel 13 (PBS)
KXTA, Channel 21 (Independent)
KUVN, Channel 23 (Univision)
KOPF, Channel 26 (Independent)
KDFI, Channel 27 (MyTV)
KMPX, Channel 29 (Spanish)
KDAF, Channel 33 (CW)
KJJM, Channel 34 (Independent)
KXTX, Channel 39 (Telemundo)
KTAQ, Channel 47 (Shopping/Religious)
KSTR, Channel 49 (Telefutura)
KFWD, Channel 52 (Independent)
KLDT, Channel 54 (Shopping)
KDTX, Channel 58 (Trinity)
KPXD, Channel 68 (Ion)
KTXA, Channel 21 (Independent)

HOUSES OF WORSHIP

Texas is one of the most churchgoing states in the nation. At least 55 percent of Texans are reported to formally adhere to a religion, according to a Churches and Church Membership in the United States 2000 survey noted in the *Texas Almanac*, though these estimates are expected to be somewhat low.

The Dallas/FortWorth Metroplex is part of the "Bible Belt," and the area is filled with churches, synagogues, temples, and mosques. They number in the thousands and are far too numerous to list here. Instead, there are numerous directories online that can help you find just the right house of worship that you are looking for.

LIVING IT UP IN TEXAS

Tobacco Laws
Smoking bans have gained popularity across the country in recent years, and DFW is no exception. Here, smoking ordinances vary by city, but are constantly changing. In general,

if you're a nonsmoker, you're likely to have a lovely time in this area. If you're a smoker, assume wherever you're going that you will not be able to smoke inside, and if you actually end up seeing an ashtray, it will be a pleasant surprise. If you like to light up right after a meal, hunt for restaurants with patios, and if you're a "smoke while you drink" smoker, stick to Fort Worth nightlife.

In Fort Worth, smoking is allowed in standalone bars, bingo halls, and outdoor dining areas more than 20 feet from a primary entrance, and also in retail tobacco shops. Smoking is prohibited in public places, including, but not limited to: restaurants, bars inside restaurants, bowling alleys, business offices and buildings, and within 20 feet of a primary entrance/exit of a regulated facility.

In the City of Dallas, smoking is banned in public buildings, restaurants, bars, pool halls (pretty much anything indoors), and even outdoors within 15 feet of a workplace entrance, except entrances leading to an outdoor deck or patio—many restaurants and bars that feature a patio do allow smoking in those areas. Tobacco shops and cigar bars are exempt from the ban.

In Arlington, smoking is allowed only in bars, nightclubs, sexually oriented businesses, billiard halls, bingo parlors, and bowling centers if: the establishment does not allow any person under the age of 18 to enter; does not open into a restaurant, hotel, or motel; and is fully enclosed from floor to ceiling by solid walls with a stand-alone heating/ventilation air conditioning system. There is a 50-foot "no smoking" arc outside each entrance and operable window of a nonsmoking facility.

Plano only allows smoking in retail tobacco stores and outdoor places, except within 25 feet of any door or operable window.

Individual penalties for breaking these laws can come with fines up to $2,000 depending on the city, so if you have any doubts, ask before lighting up.

Alcohol Consumption Laws

Texas has a mix of dry, wet, and partially dry counties, and the cities within them also vary. For that matter, the retailer and type of retailer that sells the alcohol determines the hours in which it can be sold. Generalizations are as follows:

BARS OR RESTAURANTS
Monday through Saturday, 10 AM–2 AM
Sunday, 12 PM–12 AM (10 AM–12 PM, only in conjunction with the service of food)

GROCERY STORES, CONVENIENCE STORES, OR OFF-PREMISE CONSUMPTION
Monday through Friday, 7 AM–12 AM
Saturday, 7 AM–1 AM
Sunday, 12 PM–12 AM

LIQUOR STORES
Monday through Saturday, 10 AM–9 PM
Closed on Sundays
Closed on Thanksgiving Day, Christmas Day, and New Year's Day, but if any of those days
    fall on a Sunday, then they are closed on Monday, the following day, as well.

FESTIVALS, FAIRS, CONCERTS, OR SPORTS VENUES
Regular hours plus 10 AM on Sunday

WINERIES
Monday through Saturday, 8 AM–12 AM
Sunday, 10 AM–12 AM
Regardless of purchase time or location, a person may not consume or even possess with
intent to consume an alcoholic beverage in public during these times:
Monday through Saturday, before 7 AM or after 2:15 AM
Sunday, before 12 PM or after 2:15 AM, unless it is an exception listed above.

OPEN CONTAINER LAWS
All previously opened containers of alcohol must be transported in a vehicle's trunk where
the driver and passengers do not have access.

Gun Laws
You may have heard that Texans love their guns. Before you get trigger-happy, you should
know that a permit is required to carry a handgun in Texas, and there are still several
places it is unlawful to carry a handgun, even for a licensed holder. These prohibited
places include government courts, bars (or any business that derives 51 percent or more of
its income from the sale of alcohol for on-premises consumption), a school or school
sporting event, professional sporting events, hospitals, amusement parks, race tracks,
places of worship, and many hotel lobbies. It is also unlawful for a handgun license holder
to carry a handgun while intoxicated or for the holder to intentionally fail to conceal the
handgun. (Please note: This information is meant for general purposes only; firearms laws
frequently change.)

Index